Going into Medical Practice

Compliments of
3M Pharmaceuticals

Going into Medical Practice

Rebecca B. Campen, M.D., J.D.

For medical students,
residents in training in all medical fields,
and physicians changing their practice setting
or making their practice more efficient

b
**Blackwell
Science**

© 2002 by Blackwell Science, Inc.

Editorial Offices:
Commerce Place, 350 Main Street, Malden, Massachusetts 02148, USA
Osney Mead, Oxford OX2 0EL, England
25 John Street, London WC1N 2BS, England
23 Ainslie Place, Edinburgh EH3 6AJ, Scotland
54 University Street, Carlton, Victoria 3053, Australia

Other Editorial Offices:
Blackwell Wissenschafts-Verlag GmbH, Kurfürstendamm 57, 10707 Berlin, Germany
Blackwell Science KK, MG Kodenmacho Building, 7-10 Kodenmacho Nihombashi, Chuo-ku, Tokyo 104, Japan
Iowa State University Press, A Blackwell Science Company, 2121 S. State Avenue, Ames, Iowa 50014-8300, USA

Distributors:

The Americas
Blackwell Publishing
c/o AIDC, P.O. Box 20
50 Winter Sport Lane
Williston, VT 05495-0020
(Telephone orders: 800-216-2522;
 fax orders: 802-864-7626)

Australia
Blackwell Science Pty, Ltd.
54 University Street
Carlton, Victoria 3053
(Telephone orders: 03-9347-0300;
 fax orders: 03-9349-3016)

Outside The Americas and Australia
Blackwell Science, Ltd.
c/o Marston Book Services, Ltd.
P.O. Box 269, Abingdon
Oxon OX14 4YN, England
(Telephone orders: 44-01235-465500;
 fax orders: 44-01235-465555)

All rights reserved. No part of this book may be reproduced in any form or by any electronic or mechanical means, including information storage and retrieval systems, without permission in writing from the publisher, except by a reviewer who may quote brief passages in a review.

Acquisitions: Beverly Copland
Development: Amy Nuttbrock
Production: Shawn Girsberger
Manufacturing: Lisa Flanagan

Marketing Manager: Toni Fournier
Cover design by Leslie Haimes
Typeset by Software Services
Printed and bound by Sheridan Books

Printed in the United States of America
02 03 04 05 5 4 3 2 1

The Blackwell Science logo is a trade mark of Blackwell Science Ltd., registered at the United Kingdom Trade Marks Registry

Library of Congress Cataloging-in-Publication Data

Campen, Rebecca B.
  Going into medical practice / author, Rebecca B. Campen.
     p. ; cm.
  ISBN 0-632-04621-X (pbk.)
  1. Medicine—Practice.
  [DNLM: 1. Practice Management, Medical—organization & administration.
W 80 C194g 2002] I. Title.

This book is dedicated to Christy, Brad, and Bud

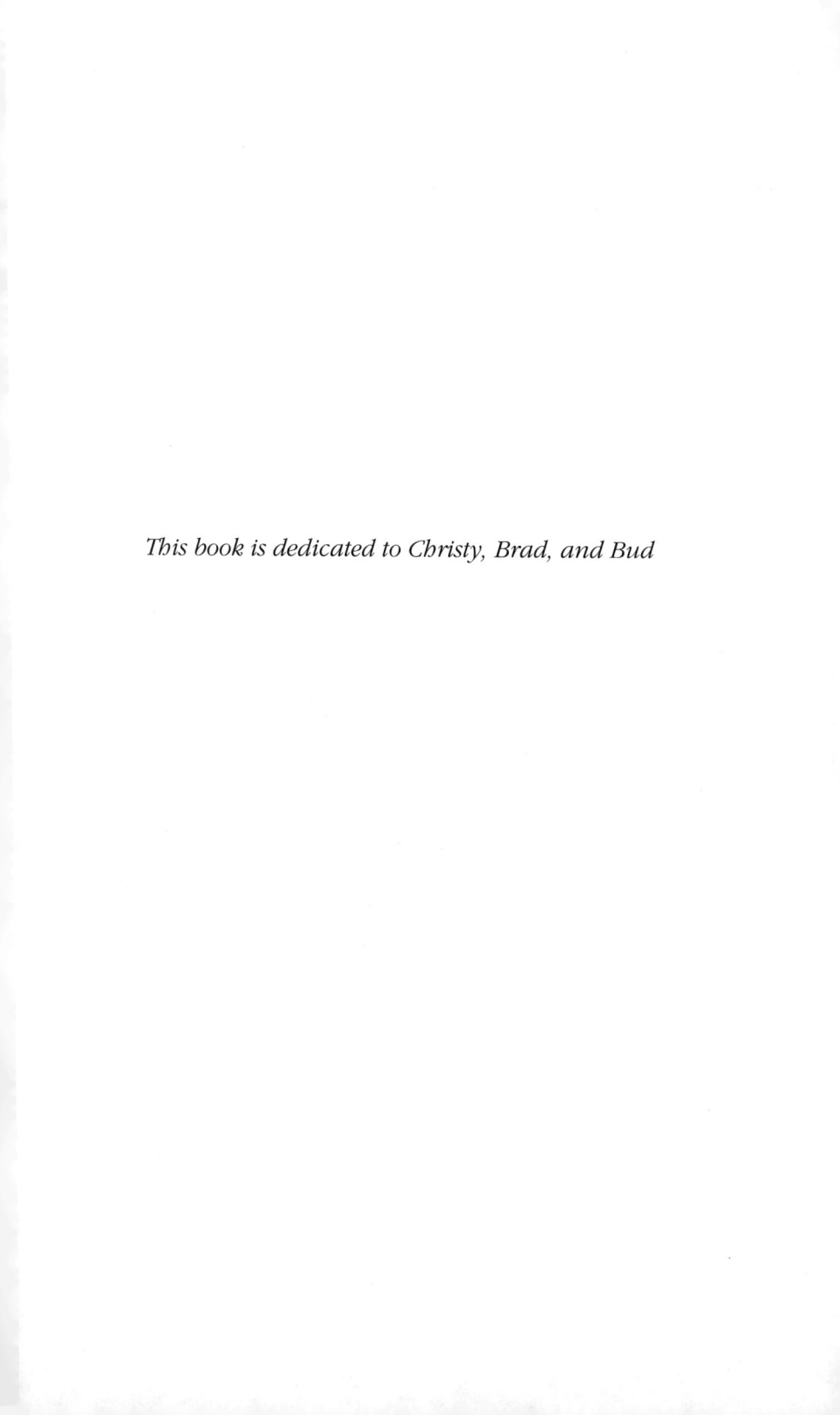

Contents

CHAPTER 1	The Beginning Is in Sight!....................	1
CHAPTER 2	Early Considerations........................	3
CHAPTER 3	Working with Someone Else.................	7
CHAPTER 4	Considerations of Opening Your Own Practice...	13
CHAPTER 5	Steps in Opening Your Own Office............	19
CHAPTER 6	Your Office Equipment and Furnishings........	39
CHAPTER 7	Employees...............................	45
CHAPTER 8	Managed Care Contracts, Blue Cross/Blue Shield, Medicare, and Medicaid...............	51
CHAPTER 9	Coding...................................	57
CHAPTER 10	Running Your Office.......................	63
CHAPTER 11	Handling Difficult Patients..................	81
CHAPTER 12	Health Care Compliance with Federal Regulations...............................	85
CHAPTER 13	Legal and Ethical Considerations: Avoiding Liability..........................	97
CHAPTER 14	Insurance................................	101
CHAPTER 15	Academic Medicine........................	105
CHAPTER 16	Enjoying Your Practice.....................	107
APPENDIX A	Suggested Reading: Books on Practice Management.......................	109
APPENDIX B	Helpful Web Sites..........................	111
ABOUT THE AUTHOR		115
INDEX		117

vii

Acknowledgments

I am very grateful to my mother and father, Mr. and Mrs. Fred Birchmore, for their encouragement in writing this book and for my mother's long hours of editing and adding her ideas from her experience in setting up a medical office. I am also grateful to my sister, Dr. Melinda Musick, for her wise input into this book, to my husband, Dr. Thomas Campen, for his encouragement and counseling, and to my three children, Christy Bedingfield, Esq., Dr. Marvin Bradford Bedingfield, and Herbert Marvin Bedingfield, Esq., who were the inspiration for writing this book.

I would also like to thank Dr. Arthur Sober, Dr. Nanette Kwon, Dr. David Wrone, Scott Kraeuter, Esq., Andrea Vadnais, Pat Sullivan and others who have made helpful suggestions for this book. Their efforts have made this book possible. I would also like to thank Beverly Copland, my editor, as well as Amy Nuttbrock, Shawn Girsberger, David Barnes, and Kathleen Mulcahy at Blackwell Science for their skill, precision, and enormous help in making this book happen.

Preface

There is a time in your medical training when important questions arise about going into practice. Where should you practice? Should you go into practice by yourself or look for a job with an established group? If you want at least to start with an established group, what arrangement is right for you? How can you negotiate a good position? How can you effectively evaluate an offered contract? If you think that you may want to set up your own practice, what is involved and is it feasible for you?

There are many different possible practice settings, and any of these can work for you. It is important to know the benefits of each, and to understand that you can set up your own practice if you choose.

This book is an introduction to going into medical practice, a framework for you to build upon as you tailor your situation to fit your needs and wishes. Use the Web references cited throughout the book to learn more[1] and to continue to update your knowledge of practice development and management. There are also rich resources available to you through your specialty association, specialty journals, and continuing medical education courses. Take an active role in your specialty association to continue to learn and protect and promote good practice of medicine. The rewards to you and to your patients will be great. I wish you luck and enjoyment of the years ahead!

---

[1] Web citations are as of the publishing of this book and may change.

CHAPTER 1

The Beginning Is in Sight!

You thought it would never happen, but it's almost here: After years of learning anatomy and pathology and everything else having to do with every microscopic part of the body. After endless diseases to learn, facts to memorize, exams to pass, patients to care for, sleepless nights on call in the hospital. Your friends in the outside world long ago bought their new cars and their houses while you have spent years just trying to pay the rent each month. And now there are those student loans to pay off.

Well, it's almost over, and the beginning is in sight. You can finally start thinking about paying off your growing mountain of debt. You will soon be able get a good night's sleep. You will even be able to plan weekends away from the hospital and be able to afford to actually take a trip somewhere. Daylight is dawning; hope is beginning to rise. You are completing your medical training.

You'll put off any decisions until closer to the time that you'll finish the residency, you say, feeling the rush of excitement of a new life dawning. You don't *care* what you do. It's almost over! You'll finally make some money. You'll finally have a life.

But wait. You do have some decisions ahead. Keep that exhilaration, but use some of that energy to consider some things that you'll need to know. Many of these points you won't learn in your residency unless you seek out the information. But your residency is actually the best time to learn these things. Before you finish and head out into the real world, read this book and consider the steps that you will need to take before you go into practice. You will be glad you did.

For those of you who are already in practice but working for someone else and thinking about starting your practice, read on.

You will find the steps you need to get on your way to having your own office.

> **Key Point**
> - Your residency is the best learning ground for going into practice.

CHAPTER 2

Early Considerations

WHERE DO YOU WANT TO PRACTICE?

You may already know where you will work. You may have a relative eagerly waiting for you to come home to join the practice. If not, decide in what part of the country you would like to live, and then come up with possible cities or towns. You will have your own personal and practical factors to consider, such as a spouse's job, family responsibilities, or children's educational needs. You may want to be close to family or you may want to explore another part of the country.

When you come up with good candidate areas for practice, investigate the physician/patient ratio for your medical specialty in those areas. You can look in the yellow pages of the phone book to find the number of specialists and compare this with the population for the area. The local Chamber of Commerce[1] can usually give you information on population, per capita income, and local industries. Talk with local physicians to learn the types and prevalence of medical insurance coverage provided and to understand the needs, challenges, and benefits of the area. The American Medical Association (AMA)[2] and the state or local medical society[3] can also provide valuable information. Visit the local hospitals and meet the CEOs; tell them that you are interested in practicing in the community, and ask about the need for physicians in your particular specialty. Drive around the residential neighborhoods to consider where you might want to live.

FINDING A JOB

Do you want to set up your own office or work for someone else? There are benefits to each. Working for someone else can have advantages. Depending upon your contract, you likely will have a salary that you can count on each month, including incentive pay. You won't have to wait until you have built up a patient base before earning a reliable income. You won't have to make an initial outlay of money to buy or rent equipment, rent an office, and pay staff. You won't have to worry about managing staff, developing policies, handling office accounting, or other functions that go with running an office. What's more, you'll have an opportunity to learn on the job how to run an office in case later you should decide to set up your own office.

Sounds like a good deal? It is, but there are other things to consider. When you work for someone else, you give up some autonomy. You won't have as much control over the hours and days that you work. You may not be able to schedule your vacation when you like. You will have less control over which and how many patients you see. You may come into the practice expecting to perform a certain procedure but not have the opportunity because another member of the practice likes to take all patients needing that procedure. You will have less control over how the office is run and which personnel are hired and fired. It is also very likely that there will be less money for you in the long run than if you go solo.

If you set up your own office, there are many benefits. You have autonomy. You control the show. You decide what hours to work, what days to take off, who to hire, who to fire, which procedures you want to handle and which you want to refer to others. You likely will make more money in the long run than if you work for someone else. If you decide to relocate, you will have an asset that you can sell and use the proceeds to set up another office.

There are downsides. You need to invest money and time to get started. There will be a lag time between the work you do and receiving payment. You will need to learn the ropes, including how to sign up with managed care companies, how to run the office, how to withhold taxes, how to do payroll, how to bill. You will probably need to outsource a lot of these duties initially, creating more up-front expenses and less income. You will need to rent an office, buy equipment, hire staff, secure a business license, and set up an accounting system. A lot of work goes into starting an office, but it's extremely satisfying and rewarding to have your own office.

A third option is to buy an existing practice, with administrative functions and patients already in place. The initial outlay will be greater than starting your own office, but the total purchase price can often be spread over a two- or three-year period, in the form of an initial partial payment plus a percentage of monthly office gross receipts. If you do decide to purchase a practice, be sure to secure an accountant or attorney to evaluate the practice and help you with the negotiations.

> **Key Points**
>
> - If you work for someone else, you will have a regular salary, you won't have to worry about running an office, and you can learn on the job about running an office should you decide later to open your own office.
> - If you work for someone else, you will have less autonomy, less control over which patients you see and which procedures you perform, and you will make less money in the long run than if you have your own practice.
> - If you have your own office, you will make more money in the long run, you will be able to decide what hours and days to work, who to hire, who to fire, which procedures to perform, and you will have assets to carry with you if you relocate.
> - If you have your own office, you will need to invest money and time initially, there will be a lag time until money comes in, and you will need to learn to set up and run an office.

ENDNOTES

1. www.uschamber.com has information about many of the U.S. Chambers of Commerce. Follow up with a call to the Chamber of Commerce in the town in which you would like to locate.
2. Contact the AMA Web site at www.ama-assn.org.
3. Members of the AMA can log onto the AMA website at www.ama-assn.org for a list of state and county medical societies across the country.

CHAPTER 3

Working with Someone Else

Let's first consider working for someone else. You may already have a job lined up or contacts that look promising. If you have no prospects yet, you will need to start looking now. If you are interested in staying in the area where you are now in training, ask your attending physicians if they know of practice opportunities. Check the ads in your specialty journals. Review the job opportunity section of your specialty association's Web site. Send out letters and an up-to-date curriculum vitae to all physicians in your specialty in the area where you would like to practice.

Recruiters can also be helpful and often send out notices about practice opportunities. Compensation for their services is usually paid by the employer but can be costly. In such cases this may influence the amount that a physician practice is willing to offer to a physician recruited to the practice.

There are many different types of practice settings to investigate, including single-specialty groups, large multi-specialty groups, HMOs, PPOs, hospital-owned clinics, and private practice settings. The larger managed care organizations are more likely to offer greater benefits than private practice settings but may have expectations that you will see a larger number of patients, as well as greater restrictions on patient referral and certain services that you can offer to a patient. Each organization is different, however, and you may find the ideal situation for you among any of these entities. See Chapter 8 for more information about managed care. There is the potential for working full time, part time, or as locum tenens in these settings. Think carefully about what situation will work best for you, and in your interviews be up-front about your preferences.

Let's say that you have found a practice that is interested in you, and you are also interested. An interview is scheduled. You have

7

planned what you will wear to the interview; your clothes are pressed and waiting. Where should you focus during the interview?

THE INTERVIEW

You are confident of your appearance, confident of your medical skills. You are ready and eager to answer any questions that the interviewer may have for you. Your attention should be directed toward the practice to determine its needs and how you can fill those needs as well as your own. This is your opportunity to determine whether this is the right practice for you by finding out some key facts about the practice. What medical problems are treated within the practice; what problems are referred out of the practice? From how large a geographic area does the practice obtain its patients? Are referrals from other physicians a large source of patients? Are billing and collections done within the practice, or is a billing company utilized? What are the laboratory capabilities of the practice? How old is the practice? Is it growing? How many patients are seen on an average day? What procedures are done? What specialized equipment is available? With which hospitals and managed care organizations are the practice physicians affiliated?

THE AGREEMENT

The interview has gone well. The interviewers have told you that they will contact you in the near future. A week later you receive a call from the practice manager. The practice is interested in you and would like to discuss terms of employment. They send you a draft contract to review.

You have a real contract! You will make money—more money than you have ever made. But in your mind a voice tells you to be careful. You know that there are things that you should watch out for in a contract. But what are they?

Look first at the compensation description. Is it reasonable in view of what you know from your colleagues about the going rate? Is there incentive compensation? Incentive pay, if adequate, can be a great morale booster when patient loads are high. If there is incentive compensation, is it based on a percentage of your gross collected income in the practice or on your net collected income? There is a big difference. Expenses are deducted from gross income before arriving at net income. Such expenses can vary widely and are under the control of the practice to a certain extent, influencing your net collected income. Of course gross collected income can also be affected by the practice. Gross collected income is dependent upon how effectively the practice billing personnel collect payment for your services, how many paying patients you have seen, and how many procedures you have performed, all of which are influenced by the practice needs and preferences. Factor in these considerations when you look at the overall compensation package offered.

Are other benefits offered such as health, dental, malpractice (professional liability), disability, and life insurance? Will you receive vacation time with pay, and if so, how much? Will you be given time off with pay and reimbursement for medical meetings? Does the practice offer a retirement plan? Will the practice pay for your state medical license and for your moving expenses? Will you receive time off with pay for illness? Will the practice allow you a budget for buying medical books for your office? What support staff will be available to you? Will the practice pay your professional dues? Will you have the opportunity to acquire equity in the practice, and if so, when and under what conditions? Is buy-in required? If so, how much will this cost? What type of equity would you acquire? Consider the answers in view of whether you would be sharing equitably in the income of the practice or whether you would be supporting older partners as they retire. What access will you have to specialized equipment that you will need in your practice? Will you be given a pager?

If malpractice insurance is offered, what kind will be provided? "Occurrence-based" malpractice insurance covers you for *events* that occur during the period of insurance. "Claims made" insurance provides coverage for *claims made* only during the period of policy coverage. If your employer provides you with claims made insurance during your time with the practice, and you later decide to leave the practice, your insurance will terminate, leaving you with an unprotected tail period. You will need to purchase "tail coverage," which is very expensive. The best alternative if you are

WORKING WITH SOMEONE ELSE   9

going into a practice that provides only claims made insurance is to negotiate up front with the practice to provide such tail coverage to you or to provide you with occurrence-based insurance, which does not require tail coverage.

Some small offices do not offer many benefits. If you do not see certain benefits listed in the contract, clarify up front with the practice whether these are offered or not, and if so, write these into the contract. If they are not offered, consider this in evaluating the compensation package presented.

Remember that a contract represents an agreement between parties. You do not have to simply accept or reject a presented contract. Mark it up as it is acceptable to you, adding your initials and the date for any changes that you make. Be sure to make a clean copy of the unmarked contract first, in case you want to go back and change what you have written into the contract.

Does the contract indicate that you will be an employee or an independent contractor? As an employee you will receive certain benefits such as having taxes deducted from your paycheck and having certain tax contributions made by the practice. As an independent contractor you will not have employee benefits. No taxes will be deducted from your paycheck, and tax contributions will not be made by the practice. You will be responsible for estimating your income for each tax year and for paying quarterly your own federal, state, and local taxes, based on your estimated income.

Read the contract carefully, and don't make any assumptions. Understand what you and the practice have agreed upon, and make sure that this agreement is in writing. The law presumes that if a physician signs a contract, he or she has read and understands every word, even the small print. Rely on an attorney with expertise in physician employment contracts to review your contract. Ask your colleagues for a recommendation of an attorney or call your state bar association. The money spent will be well worthwhile. The attorney will be more likely to recognize hidden pitfalls. For example, who owns the building that houses the practice? Who owns the office equipment? Does the practice rent from a third party or do the members of the practice personally own the building (or office equipment) and lease back to their incorporated practice? The rent is a practice expense, affecting net income of the practice. If your contract specifies that you will receive a percentage of net income collected, determine what expenses will be deducted to arrive at the net collected amount. Consider the following scenario: The present partners own the building that houses the practice (or equipment used by the practice) and they determine the amount of rent that the practice pays. The partners will, therefore, recoup the rent that the practice pays. If your incentive pay is based on net income and a portion of rent is deducted to arrive at net income, you will be the one affected by the rent. Should you become a partner down the road, you might find that you are the only one in the practice really paying rent if the other partners decline to invite you to buy into the building or set the buy-in at an impossible amount. These may be worst-case scenarios, but be aware of such possibilities and have your attorney review the contract and add any clarifying sections necessary for your protection.

Clarify the practice's expectations for you in return for your compensation. What are the office hours? Are Saturday office hours expected, and if so, how often? What nighttime and weekend on-call time is expected? Will you be given time for handling administrative matters? How many patients will you be expected to see each day? How much time will be allowed for seeing new or return patients? Will all physicians in the practice share night and consult call time equally? What is the term, or length of employment, specified by the contact? What if you decide that you want out of the contract? What provisions are included for termination? What notification period is required?

Does the contract contain a non-compete clause? This limits your ability to see and treat patients within a certain radius of the practice for a certain period of time after you leave employment of the practice. The clause may specify that you may not treat patients of the practice for that certain period of time, regardless of where you locate. Such clauses reflect a practice's natural concern to not lose its patients to its departing physicians, but can restrict your ability to practice in the same locality. Courts in different states differ in the extent to which non-compete provisions are upheld. It is important to ask your attorney to review such provisions in view of the prevailing laws in your area. If you are thinking of eventually starting your practice in a certain area but want to work as an employee for the first few years, it would be best to work outside of the area where you plan to locate your office.

If you have made changes to the contract that are not accepted by the practice or if you have questions that are not answered to your satisfaction, you will need to negotiate. Have clearly in mind what you must have and what you would like to have. Hold fast to the former, and give up some of the latter if necessary in the negotiations. Your attorney can be very helpful in negotiations; at least indicate that you must check with him or her before making any final decisions.

Key Points

- Examine an employment contract to determine whether compensation is sufficient, whether there is incentive pay, and if so, whether incentive pay is based on gross collected income.
- See whether there are other benefits, including malpractice insurance, as well as whether there is a non-compete clause.

CHAPTER 4

Considerations of Opening Your Own Practice

Now let's consider opening your own practice. You know the area in which you would like to locate, and from your residency experience you believe that you know how best you can see patients and what sort of staff support will be most useful to you, but how would you set up the administrative functions of the practice? You know that your expertise is in your medical specialty area and not in setting up offices. And how could you afford to set up an office with the mountain of debt accumulated from your medical training? Would it really be worth all of the trouble?

MANAGING THE COST OF SETTING UP AN OFFICE

Let's first talk about how to manage the cost of setting up an office. There are several ways to do this. First, you can take a business plan to a bank in the locality of your office and ask for a loan. Determine how much you will need to borrow to open your own office. Look through supply catalogs and determine the cost of supplies and equipment that you will need for the first year of practice. Include the cost of an office to rent, estimation of phone and utilities, cost of staff, cost of answering/scheduling services, cost of accounting and billing services, and your own salary needs for the first year. Also include cost of malpractice and other insurance. A well-constructed plan with reasonable estimates will be extremely helpful in securing a loan adequate for establishing your own practice. Your loan payback will be based on the assumption that your practice must build before you can achieve stable income.

Second, you can commute to a practice in another town and use part of your income to gradually acquire the minimum of supplies and equipment that you will need to start a practice in your own locality. You must locate your office in a town far enough away from your employer's office so that you do not take patients away from his or her practice and so that he or she does not feel threatened that this might happen. You must be up front with your employer at the time of your hiring, so that he or she can decide whether this arrangement will be satisfactory prior to the signing of the contract. During the weekends when you are not working, you can check into potential office spaces in your locality, such as a time share that might be available to you one half day, with the possibility of expanding utilization of the time share as your practice builds. Time-share offices are offered by some hospitals and may include administrative or medical assistant staff as part of the fee that you pay for use of the office. You can also check into renting another physician's office on his or her day off. As your own practice builds, you can decrease the days that you work for your employer, according to the provisions of your contract, and you can then rent your own office instead of the time-share office.

Third, in some communities needing a physician in your specialty, the local hospital may offer loans or guarantees of compensation to help the physician establish a practice in that community. Talk with the local hospitals to determine whether there is such a need and such help in financing a start-up practice. It is important to have your attorney carefully review any such contracts offered before signing.

REQUIREMENTS FOR OPENING YOUR OWN OFFICE

Before getting into the details of opening an office, let's take a bird's-eye view of what's involved. You need to start working on opening your office at least six months ahead of your planned opening date. You will need to apply for a state medical license as early as possible. You must get on staff early at the hospitals with which you would like to affiliate, so you should apply for hospital privileges at least six months prior to your practice start date. Personnel in the hospitals can help you find an office, hire out your billing, and advertise your practice. They can also put you on their speaker's forum (public service) for the community to get to know you. You need to contact the health care plans in your practice community at least six months ahead to start the process of joining the plans as a provider. This is important—you've got to be on the health care plans to make money, but first you must have your state medical license and often an office address, so you have to think and act ahead.

You will need a business license once you have an office address; you will need to check with your local city hall to apply for this license. You will need a Clinical Laboratory Improvement Amendments (CLIA) certificate and you will need an Occupational Safety and Health Administration (OSHA) plan to carry out that conforms to OSHA regulations. An OSHA kit to help you with this can be ordered from most supply catalogs. Information about CLIA[1] and OSHA[2] can be obtained readily from the Internet. You should also have a compliance plan for your office. These requirements will be discussed in more detail in later chapters.

You will need to decide where to locate your office and to secure an office in this location. You should locate your office where it is easy to find. A sign that is visible from the street is very useful in letting people know about your office. You will need to determine how many people you will hire in your office. You can start with just one or two until your practice builds. You will need to decide what office hours to keep. This is your choice; you may want to add some late hours and a few Saturdays to build up your practice. You will need to decide who will schedule your patients when you first open your office and are not there every day. There are scheduling services that you can hire; ask whether the scheduling service will charge you by the hour or by the number of patients scheduled. You will need to select an answering service. Some answering services will also schedule patients for you. You will need to think about how to advertise your practice. You can send out announcements to the staff of the hospital(s) with which you affiliate. The hospital public relations office will help you with this. You can also participate in public services through the hospital, such as screening clinics and public outreach programs, to let people know that you are establishing a practice in the community.

You will need to make arrangements for billing and collections for the patient visits to your office. You can outsource this at first, but make sure that the billing company is reputable. Plan to incorporate this into your office functions as soon as possible. It is vital that you learn to code correctly before you leave your residency-training program, and you should learn the mechanisms of billing and collections, as well. If you join a medical practice as an employee with plans to open your own office later, learn everything that you can from that practice about the coding, billing, and collection process.

You will need to determine what supplies you will require as you start your practice. Order your supplies and equipment early, and store them at home if necessary. Start with a small number of everything that you will need. There are companies that will ship overnight in case you run short.[3] Get catalogs from the technical exhibits when you attend your annual Academy meeting and browse through them, making a list of what you will need—you'll be surprised at the number of things necessary, from alcohol swabs to an autoclave. Think about a normal day of seeing patients and think about everything that you reach for during that day. Try to order what you can from the technical exhibit booths of your specialty association meetings—it's all there and you'll save time and know what you are getting.

You will need to buy or rent office furniture for your office. To obtain the best deals on office furniture for starting your office, check the want ads for retiring physicians who are selling their office furniture, as well as office equipment stores that have used office furniture. You can find some very good furniture at very reasonable prices.

You won't make any money for the first several months—although you'll be spending it—so save ahead or moonlight in another medical office (far distant from yours) until your office is up and running and bringing in income.

You'll need to secure malpractice insurance early in the process. You will need to develop patient encounter forms and other administrative forms for your office. Study the ones that are used in your residency program or in other medical offices and tailor your own to fit your needs. You will need to determine fee schedules and advertise your practice. You will need to hire an accountant and develop an office accounting system. You will need to evaluate computer systems and software for your patient information and accounting. Look at the systems that other offices in your medical specialty use and ask the administrative personnel in those offices about their computer systems. Do your own research before you consider buying a system, no matter how good an advertised system looks.

This sounds like a lot, and there's still more to come, but having your own office is definitely worth the effort.

Key Points

- To manage the cost of setting up an office, develop a business plan and secure a business loan.
- Consider starting your office part-time while practicing with a group distant from your own office location.
- In some communities, the local hospital may offer loans or compensation guarantees to help you establish a practice in that community.
- Obtain an overall view of what is involved in opening an office.

ENDNOTES

1. The Clinical Laboratory Improvement Amendments (CLIA) are described at www.hcfa.gov/medicaid/clia/cliahome.htm or www.phppo.cdc.gov/dls/clia, and are further discussed in this book.
2. www.osha.gov.
3. There are many companies such as Henry Schein (www.henryschein.com) that will give quick delivery.

CHAPTER 5

Steps in Opening Your Own Office

We've already discussed some of the things to do in setting up your office, but let's start again, step by step. We'll divide the steps into phase I, phase II, and phase III. Phase I will not require any outlay of money, except the cost of a medical license, and will let you decide whether you want to do this or not; while you are deciding, you are making progress toward your goal. You *will* want to do this once you get started.

PHASE I

As mentioned previously, it is very important to start phase I early—at least six months before you plan to open your office—and phase II should be started at least three months ahead of time. Be sure to keep track of all expenses associated with starting your office, as well as moving expenses, so that you can discuss with your accountant what items are tax deductible.

Step 1
Apply for a medical license in the state where you want to practice. Call the state medical society for the address and phone number of your state Board of Medical Examiners or state Medical Licensing Board for information about how to apply for the license.[1] You will need to attach copies of documents such as medical school diploma and certification of passing the National Board of Medical Examiners Exam (NBME)[2] or the Federal Licensing Exam (FLEX),[3] or Educational Commission for Foreign Medical Graduates Exam (ECFMG).[4] Check with the licensing board of

your state to determine whether the exam that you took will qualify you for certification in your state. Keep a medical document file of all of the documents that you are required to attach to your application for your medical license. You will need to submit the documents with various other applications, for example, as you apply for hospital staff privileges and to be a provider for health care plans. It's best if you have a complete file so that you do not have to assemble the documents each time that you file an application. Apply for a Drug Enforcement Administration (DEA) license.[5] Keep a copy of this license in your medical document file. The DEA license is a federal license that must be renewed. Some states also require a state DEA license. Check with your state medical society or state licensing board to determine whether a state DEA license is required in your state. See Appendix B for the Web site of the five schedules of controlled drugs and Chapter 10 for more information about prescribing controlled substances.

Step 2
Determine your target date for opening your office. Make it realistic. You will need to allow at least six months to become a provider for health insurance plans and to set up your office.

Step 3
Decide where you want to locate your office. Determine the number and locations of the physicians in your specialty within a reasonable distance from the area where you would like to live. Get a detailed city map from the Chamber of Commerce, and mark on the map where those physicians are located to get an idea of optimal practice locations that are not too close to your colleagues. Check with the local hospital(s) to find time-share offices where you could locate your practice at first. Drive around the areas that you think would be optimal and notice traffic flow, proximity to other physician offices and medical complexes, and how close they are to diagnostic laboratories and x-ray facilities. Consider the safety and quality of the neighborhood. Consider proximity to public transportation. Avoid an office that requires climbing steps to enter. Look for offices for rent in the area and call to find out the price, the square footage of the property, and whether the landlord

would build the interior to your office needs (paint, add rugs, and build exam rooms to your specifications). You are just collecting information at this stage, but when you become really interested in a property, obtain from the relevant realtor a copy of the lease form that would be used and review it. Check with the hospital in the area to find out if any doctors are retiring. You might find not only great office space, but you might also be able to acquire used office furniture of excellent quality with which to start your office.

Step 4

Determine what office equipment and supplies you will need. Get supply catalogs for physicians in your specialty and go through them page by page, putting a check by the items that you will need to get started. You can find many health care supply companies on the Internet that will be happy to mail their catalog to you. You will need your specialty instruments, exam tables, lights, at least one chair in each of the exam rooms and chairs in the waiting room. You will need an autoclave and solutions for cleaning instruments and for wiping down tabletops and exam tables. Check your catalogs for appropriate cleaning solutions. You will need at least two small refrigerators; one for specimens and one for you and your staff to store your lunch. Plan for a microwave and a small table for eating lunch in a room in the back. Consider adding a portable television that plays videotapes to your office; this can keep children happy and can also be used for educating your patients about medical problems. Your specialty association will have educational tapes that you can purchase for this purpose or you can make your own.

Depending upon your specialty, you will likely need gauze, syringes, alcohol swabs, cotton balls, lidocaine, and other injectables. You may also want oxygen and nasal cannulas for patients who feel faint. Make a list and update it as you think of anything else that you may need. Think about what you reach for in the way of supplies and instruments when you examine a patient. Visit a friend's office outside of the area where you plan to practice and look at what your friend has in stock. Get to know the office manager in your friend's office; the office manager can be a wonderful help with questions that arise as you set up your office. You will need a fax, a small copier, and a computer. Consider renting a postage scale that will stamp mail for you with the exact postage due. This saves money and is much more convenient than applying stamps. Don't forget to have a small tape recorder if you want to dictate your progress notes. Dictating saves time when you are seeing patients, but you will then need someone to transcribe the notes. You may want to write your notes until your patient volume increases. If you do dictate your notes, be sure to jot down a few words on the progress note to remind yourself of the problem and treatment in case your patient comes back before your dictation is transcribed. Then write "Dictated" and sign your name so that if your charts are audited regarding billing compliance, it will be evident that this was not your complete note. Check into leasing possibilities for any large equipment that you will need to practice your specialty. You will read more about equipment and office furnishings in Chapter 6.

Step 5

Determine what forms you will use for patient encounters, specimen submission, informed consent, and patient information sheets. Look at the forms used where you are currently training or working in another office. Read them as if you were a patient. Are the questionnaires easy to understand and phrased in a tactful way to obtain all of the information that you need? From the patient encounter form, will you obtain as much information as possible to document past medical, family, and social history, as well as the chief complaint? Remember that you can refer to the patient encounter form in your progress note and "get credit" for documentation of these elements.[6] An updated patient encounter form is therefore important in meeting billing documentation requirements for Medicare. More about that will be covered later in Chapter 9.

Be sure to have informed consent forms for procedures and for photographs, and list on the consent forms any complications that are risks for the procedure. Patient information sheets are very important in clarifying information for the patient. You will also want to have forms explaining wound care if you do procedures, and you will want handouts that give patients more information about their illnesses. Many informational brochures are available through the academy of your specialty, but you will also want to print up some of your own. Develop a brochure to place in your waiting area that welcomes the patient to your office and describes your practice, your credentials, procedures conducted, and your commitment to the health care of your patients. List phone numbers for scheduling patients and for emergencies. Many patients will take these brochures to give to a friend, which helps to expand your patient population. You will need forms for submitting specimens to the laboratories. The laboratories that you use provide these forms, as well as specimen bottles. If your office is not in a hospital building, upon request many laboratories will attach a specimen drop box near your office back door and provide specimen pick-up services. Call the laboratories that you would like to use and arrange to have a drop box installed. Many HCFA forms, such as Clinical Laboratory Improvement Amendments (CLIA) application for certification, Medicare Participating Agreement, Certification of Necessity, and HCFA Health Insurance Claim Form (for paper filing Medicare claims) are downloadable from the Internet[7] or available through your local Regional HCFA office.

Step 6

Check into computer systems to determine what to use for billing and what software you will need. Talk with other offices about their systems. If you want to save costs at first, you can use the old pegboard system to keep track of patient billing and hire out your billing. You will need to take the pegboard ledger and copies of your notes to the biller each week for billing. You may also want to find an answering/scheduling service that will answer your phone and schedule patients for you at first when you have only a few patients and are not in the office every day. Check into pager services available in your area.

Step 7

Apply for staff privileges at the hospital(s) in your preferred office area. Contact the office of the chief executive officer (CEO) or the chief of staff to set up an appointment to discuss your wish to apply for staff privileges. Ask for information about the process of applying for staff privileges, the regulations and bylaws for hospital staff, available facilities and equipment for special procedures that you will perform in your practice, and whether the hospital administration will be willing to purchase special equipment that you may need for hospital-based procedures. If you ask for staff privileges that include performing certain procedures in the hospital, you will need to provide documentation of sufficient experience in performing such procedures as well as proof of proficiency, so be sure to keep your procedure log up-to-date throughout your residency and keep any certificates or attestations of proficiency that you have earned. Discuss your plans for locating in the community with the hospital chairman of your specialty and meet the other practitioners of your specialty in the community. The public relations department of the hospital, or its equivalent, can be very helpful as you start an office. This department may be able to help you locate an office, find someone who will be willing to do your billing or transcribe your dictation at first, help you find personnel to staff your office, and give you information about health care plans. Ask about office space that the hospital may have available for rent. They will also help you print announcements of your new practice once you have joined the staff, and the public relations department can put you in touch with the hospital-purchasing department for information about good sources for ordering your office supplies and equipment. Offer to give talks about your specialty and participate in other events that the public relations department may plan. Contact the local medical society and apply to become a member. Notify other physicians in your community that you are available for care of patients and for consults. Meet with the other physicians in your specialty to introduce yourself. Discuss with them the possibilities for sharing call.

Step 8

Secure provider numbers and required licenses. Contact Medicare,[8] Medicaid,[9] and Blue Cross[10] to sign up as a provider and to receive a provider number from each. To enroll with Medicare as a provider, you will need to look on the Medicare Web site for the agency in your state that administers part B (the physician portion) of the Medicare program. For Blue Cross, contact the Blue Cross office in your region. You can obtain information for contacting this office on the Blue Cross Web site. Contact your state agency that administers the Medicaid program in order to sign up as a provider. This information can be obtained from the Medicaid Web site. Sign up to join other health insurer groups. The hospital where you apply for privileges or other medical offices in your specialty can tell you what managed care groups are important in the area. If you are other than a primary care physician, find out whether these groups are HMOs or PPOs and whether patients will need to go through a gatekeeper and therefore require referrals to see you. You will need to contact these provider groups and get their forms to sign up to be a provider. You may be able to join the plans through a hospital organization where you have privileges. If you are already a provider of health care plans in your employer's office, you will need to call the health care plans and ask to add the location of your new office when you have your new address. Determine from the plans whether enrollment is currently open and if so, ask about the procedure for application, the regulations, and the estimated time frame for gaining approval to the plans. As already discussed, this step as well as the preceding steps should be completed at least six months before you plan to start seeing patients. You will need an office address to become a provider on plans; ask the plan if you can give a temporary address until you secure your office, and change the address with the provider when you do. You will also need an employee identification number (EIN) if you will be paying wages to one or more employees. Contact the Internal Revenue Service (IRS)[11] to apply for and obtain this number. Some states or communities require a business (occupational) license. Contact the tax collector's office in your community to determine if this is required for your community. See the Small Business Association Web site[12] for further information.

Step 9
Reserve your office phone numbers and list your office name and your primary number in both the white and the yellow pages of the phone book. You must do this even before you have your office address. New phone books usually come out in January each year, and the applications for listings for the new books usually close in the fall of the preceding year. If you wait too long,

there will be a year's delay in getting your number listed. Call the phone company and find out the deadline for getting your listing into the new phone book. Tell the phone company in what general area you will probably locate your office and ask them to assign you phone numbers for that general location. Reserve at least three phone numbers in sequence to be activated in the future. You will want to list only your primary number in the phone book. When you activate the phones in your office, your primary number will roll over to each of the other two lines in sequence so that if the primary line is busy, the second line will be activated, and if the first two lines are busy, the third line will be activated. You need sequential numbers for this to happen, so be sure to reserve the numbers. If your office is not yet open when the new phone books are distributed, you can install your primary office line in your house with voice mail to let people know that the office is not yet open and to indicate when you will begin scheduling patients. When you are ready to start scheduling patients, you can forward the line to an answering/scheduling service, and when you open your office, you can transfer the line to your office. At this time, you may want to secure an additional, unlisted line for your private use at the office.

PHASE II

Step 10
Determine how much money you will need to borrow to open your office. Add up the cost of supplies and equipment that you will need to get started, your office rent, the estimated cost of phone and utilities, the cost of the answering/scheduling service, and the cost of an office manager and any additional staff that you will need to get started. To begin, hire your staff part-time at an hourly rate when you have only a few patients. As your practice increases and you increase the number of hours that your staff works, you will need to deduct social security, pay FICA, and consider benefits for your staff.[13] You can hire a payroll service or an accountant to handle your payroll payments, deductions and tax contributions at first, and you can bring these functions in-house

as your practice grows. You will still want to keep your accountant involved to give advice, review quarterly reports, and prepare your income tax returns.

Step 11
Develop a business plan. Ask your bank for forms to apply for a business loan. In your business plan, estimate your expenses for opening and operating an office for the first year and estimate your income for each month during the first year. Don't forget to add the cost of malpractice, health, and disability insurance to the estimate of your expenses, as well as the cost of a business license.[14] Include a salary for yourself in your estimate of what you will need, since income will be slow at first. To estimate your income, you should know what billing codes you are likely to use and what reimbursement can be expected from the different insurance groups for each code. Buy a CPT[15] codebook for determining billing codes. The insurance groups can provide you with their current reimbursement amounts for office visits and procedures. You will also need to buy an International Classification of Disease (ICD)[16] codebook for diagnosis codes. Add the cost of these books, and any other books that you will need to buy for your office, to your business plan estimate of expenses.

Step 12
Apply for malpractice insurance (see Chapter 14 for more information about malpractice insurance). Your malpractice insurance should take effect the day that you open your office.

Step 13
Take your business plan and business loan application to the bank. If you are in a specialty where you do not need a lot of expensive equipment and you are generating income by working part time in other medical offices of your specialty (far away from the area where you plan to practice), you may not need to borrow much if any in order to slowly build up your office. You might, for example, initially see patients for half a day per week in a hospital time-share unit where facilities and receptionist are provided

for an hourly fee. Not all hospitals have this type of facility, but it is worth checking on as you start your practice since you could avoid having to rent an office from the beginning. As another alternative, you could rent an existing office on a physician's day off in return for giving that physician a percentage of your income generated from use of his office, plus reimbursement for office supplies used. As your patient load increases, you could move to your own office. If you do go to the bank to borrow money, consider your needs (e.g., rent, mortgage, living expenses) when deciding how much to borrow to get started.

With this step you are making a commitment to opening an office. You should now open a business account with the bank into which the office collections can be deposited once your office is up and running.

Step 14

Decide on your office space. Drive around the area where you would like to locate and look for offices for rent. In your search, note proximity to hospitals and to potentially referring physicians, and be sure that parking is adequate. Ask whether the landlord would renovate the space to accommodate your needs, including removing or installing walls, installing plumbing, installing carpeting, painting walls, and installing outlets and grounding necessary for your office equipment. Ask whether cleaning, security, pest control, and building insurance are provided. Examine the lease carefully. The term *standard lease* is misleading. Leases vary greatly. Review the lease carefully and ask an attorney to look over the lease before you sign it. Two or three years for the term of the lease is reasonable if you anticipate moving to a larger office at that time. A shorter term does not guarantee the same rent if you renew the lease. A longer term can lock you into an office after you have outgrown it. Strike out of the lease any clauses that allow the landlord to increase the rent during the term of the lease. Look at the lease to see if any utilities are provided and check to see who will pay for repairs. Make sure that any renovations or other accommodations that the landlord agrees to make are listed in the lease. Write into the lease the corrections or additions that you feel are important. Initial and date these changes to the lease. Be sure that you inspect the rental space before you open your office. Write down any damages and give the landlord a copy. You will need to have a sign made for your office if the landlord does not provide this. Arrange for utility and phone service through the relevant companies. Contact an office cleaning service to service your office if this is not provided in the lease, and contact a hazardous waste disposal service to remove your hazardous waste. Have office keys made for the staff that you will hire.

Step 15

Hire an office manager on an hourly basis. He or she will be of great assistance to you at this stage. Your office manager will be helpful in searching the want ads for used medical furniture, in ordering the supplies and equipment that you will need, and in contacting health care organizations to give your new office address. See Chapter 6 for more information about your office equipment and furnishings. Ask your office manager to learn how to code and bill for your office. As previously mentioned, you should also learn how to code and bill. Your office manager can set up an office accounting and billing system if you prefer to conduct these functions in-house instead of outsourcing, and in any event he or she should be able to cross-check if these functions are performed by others. Work with your office manager to set up a filing system for charts. Decide how you would like your charts arranged and develop with your office manager the patient encounter form, pathology specimen form, informed consent form, and any other necessary forms. There are many different types of charts and many ways to arrange them. Look in the office supply catalogs for types of charts and work with your office manager to develop the best system for you. Develop job descriptions for personnel that you plan to hire as your practice starts and as it grows. Determine how coding for office visits and procedures will be recorded, how billing will be performed (pegboard or computer), how collections will be handled, and how insurance forms will be processed. Develop your patient referral list for sending patients to other specialists. The public relations department of your local hospital can be helpful. Choose a collection agency for those patient bills down the road that your office isn't able to collect. (Do not be quick to use a collection agency—make your staff try to collect on the overdue patient bills for at least six months before turning them over to a collection agency.)

Step 16

Determine a fee schedule for your charges. You should not set your fees by another physician's fee schedule because this is considered price fixing by the federal government. You can certainly get an idea of the range of fees charged for the various services that you perform so that you can make an informed decision about the fees that you will charge. You can obtain information from the AMA that will be helpful in determining how to set your fees, and your accountant will be very helpful in this regard also. Contact Medicare, Medicaid, Blue Cross, and other carriers for prevailing fees, for insurance forms for paper billing, for information about connections for computer billing, and for current fee information. Periodically review your fee schedule to determine whether the fee that you charge is comparable to the service that you render and modify as necessary. Decide whether you will accept credit card charges for co-payments or other payments. If so, contact credit card companies to make arrangements.

Step 17

Order supplies and equipment. Determine how these orders will be received if your office is not staffed every day at first. If your office is not yet ready, rent a post office box for receiving the orders. Order the current year CPT (billing codes) and ICD (coding diagnoses) coding books. Explore leasing rather than buying expensive equipment until your office is up and running. See Chapter 6 for more information about office equipment and furnishings. Order the announcements for the opening of your office. Order your business cards (3½″ × 2″), business stationery and envelopes, insurance claim forms, return appointment cards, and prescription blanks. Order encounter sheets (coding sheets for billing purposes), stationery for sending out bills, and memo sheets with your office name, address, and phone number for giving patients instructions. Compose patient information sheets answering common patient questions. These can also be obtained from your specialty academy. Develop an office policy booklet and a welcome brochure for your office.

Step 18
Learn about federal regulations that impact medical practice (see Chapter 12) and understand correct coding (see Chapter 9). Acquire the necessary insurance for a medical office (see Chapter 14). Make sure that your insurance takes effect by the time your office opens. Understand legal and ethical issues in medical practice (see Chapter 13).

Step 19
Hire other necessary personnel. Develop employee job descriptions and ask your office manager to advertise for any additional help that you may need at first. Involve your office manager (and any other staff that you may have hired) in screening applicants, and interview the manager's top choices. Start with the smallest number of staff that you can manage with at first and add more as necessary. The office manager can act as receptionist initially, and you can hire a medical assistant and wait until your practice builds to hire additional staff. Be clear when you hire your office manager that you want him or her to take an active role in all office activities. Be sure to check references and keep records of interviews. Decide with your office manager how you would like the staff to accommodate patients as they come to the office, what staff member should remain at the reception desk, and who should be with you seeing patients. The office manager should perform one of these functions, and optimally all office staff hired should be capable of performing any function within the office. Make your policies and your expectations known up front to all potential employees during their interviews.

Step 20
Meet with your accountant to discuss the establishment of your practice as a sole proprietorship, a partnership, or a corporation. Many physicians going into practice alone start their practice as a sole proprietorship. Discuss benefits and disadvantages of each form of practice with your accountant. Also discuss setting up payroll,

reporting requirements of the Internal Revenue Service, and employee benefits. Your accountant can help you set up your accounting system and can periodically monitor its functions, as well as prepare tax reports and give financial advice. Your accountant can also be very helpful in preparing initial information, such as a net worth statement, which is important in applying for a business loan for starting your office.

Step 21

Give notice of the opening of your practice through the local newspaper and notify the medical staff at the hospital(s) where you have applied for privileges. Again, the public relations department of the hospital may be able to give advice on having announcements printed, and you can put the printed announcements in each staff physician's mailbox in the doctor's lounge of the hospital.

Step 22

Develop a scheduling system and begin scheduling patients. A scheduling/answering service can do this while your staff is not yet full-time. On days when the staff is not in the office, forward the phones to the scheduling service. Determine which days and hours you will be available for seeing patients. Consider scheduling a Saturday morning at least once a month to attract new patients. The scheduling system should be tailored to the length of time that it takes you to see initial or return patients. It is important to build flexibility into the schedule. Some offices double book patients on the hour and save a scheduling slot at the end of the hour. Others reserve scheduling slots at other times during the day. See Chapter 10 for discussion of wave scheduling. You will probably need to try several different methods to arrive at a system that works best for you and for your patients, but there will be times when even the best system does not work. When that happens, an apology by you and your staff to those made to wait longer than usual will go far in maintaining a good relationship with your patients. Have your staff call patients the day before their appointment to remind them of their appointment.

Step 23
Buy a pager, or a cellular phone with a pager, and arrange for pager service. Arrange call-sharing with others in your area in your specialty.

Step 24
Determine a collection agency that you will use as necessary and develop guidelines for when such a service would be needed. Check into potential billing services that you may want to use as your practice is starting if you do not yet have the necessary staff for billing and collecting fees. Check into temporary personnel services (temp services) to use for filling in as necessary when your office is just starting. These services are more expensive than hiring your own staff, but knowing who you can call in emergencies is very important.

PHASE III

Step 25
Think through a patient encounter. Decide how you and your staff will interact with the patient. You may want your assistant to greet the patient and lead him or her to the exam room, to discuss with the patient his or her reason for the visit and symptoms, to take vital signs, to obtain a medical history, and to ask the patient to put on an exam gown. Determine what you want your assistant to record on the chart for you to read prior to your entry into the exam room. Decide when you want your assistant to be with you in the room, and what instructions you want the assistant to give to the patient. Decide how the charts will be handled after the visit. Will you write your note or dictate in the exam room with the patient? Will you add your billing and diagnosis codes, and give the chart to the patient to take to your receptionist, or will you dictate your note after the patient leaves the exam room and turn in your charts to your receptionist at the end of the day? It is convenient to have an encounter sheet with CPT and ICD codes attached to the chart. You can check the appropriate codes depending upon the services rendered, and

the patient can bring the encounter sheet to the receptionist at the conclusion of the visit, allowing your office billing functions to proceed efficiently. You can then keep the chart for your note or dictation as necessary. See Chapter 10 for more details on patient visits, as well as other information on running your office.

Step 26
Begin seeing patients. Ask your patients for feedback on the patient encounter forms to determine if they are understandable. Be sensitive to patient privacy and avoid asking any information that is not relevant to patient care. Remember that a good rapport with your patient and informed consent are important in avoiding misunderstanding and malpractice actions.

Step 27
Become your patient's doctor. This may seem like an obvious statement, but when the patient says "my doctor," make sure that he or she says it with pride and confidence. There is a difference between "I went to see a doctor" and "I went to see my doctor." Make sure that you are available for your patients. Make them feel that you care about them, and give them your undivided attention during their visits. The length of time that you spend with them is not as important as the quality of care that you give. As your practice builds, you can have medical assistants do everything from transcribe notes to take histories and listen to problems, but avoid trimming down the time that you spend with your patients to the point that they feel that you are hardly there. You are their doctor, and they will want to know that you understand their worries. Consider these concerns carefully, and treat patients according to your best judgment. Besides simply performing these duties, it is also important to convey to your patients that you care through your careful attention to them. Arrange your schedule well in advance. A patient usually will not mind changing an appointment three weeks in advance, but too many last minute cancellations may make your patients decide to find another doctor. Understand what your patients need. Some of your patients will not have detectable medical problems but will need reassurance. Psychological problems, stress, and insecurities all factor into patient concerns. Try to

see beyond the presenting problem in order to understand these needs and treat with these factors in mind. If you do, your patients will sense that you really understand them well and will be loyal.

Step 28

Evaluate your office on an ongoing basis. Hire each of your employees for a six-month trial. Different personalities can be interesting, but in an office, reliability and efficiency are the standards by which each of your staff must be evaluated. Develop policies and standards and adhere to them. See Chapter 7 for more information about employees. Develop a compliance program (see Chapter 12) and an OSHA policy (see Chapter 12), and understand CLIA regulations (see Chapter 12). Make certain that you understand correct coding (see Chapter 9), how to bill patients and providers, and how to follow up on collections so that you can be certain that your staff is performing these functions effectively. You cannot let yourself slip into the mode of letting others handle all these duties. Your income is your lifeline, and you must understand how to code, bill, and collect to make certain they are done correctly. Have an office quality assurance (QA) meeting at least quarterly to review these functions and to answer any questions, develop any necessary policies, and discuss any issues.

Step 29

Contribute to your community. Volunteer your services in occasional medical screening clinics for the public. Participate in community education through the public relations department of the hospital where you have staff privileges. This hospital department can arrange for you to speak about new medical treatments of interest to the press. Accept invitations to talk to different groups about medical issues, problems, and treatments. Not only will these activities contribute to your community, but they will also profile your practice desirably.

Step 30

Utilize the experts. Learn from your friends who have set up offices. Gather information from many sources and then create your own office, your own forms, and your own system. Hire an accountant. While your practice is small, you may not need as much of an accountant's time as you will as your practice enlarges, but select one to help you set up your accounts and to tell you what you need to know about FICA, social security payments, and other accounting functions. A couple of hours with an accountant early in your practice will put you on the right path, and this will be a valuable contact when you need the accountant's services down the road. The same goes for an attorney. Select an attorney to review your lease agreement, or any other agreement, and to give you advice on practice arrangements and then you will have the attorney as a contact.

Step 31

Enjoy your practice. Carve out the time from your schedule that you need for other things. As your practice gains momentum and the patient load increases, be sure not to forget to give yourself some time to rest and relax. If the pace has been particularly hectic, schedule time off to go to lunch or to play an afternoon game of tennis or golf. You will find that a good balance of work and relaxation will allow you to maintain enthusiasm for your practice and your patients and to contribute significantly to your practice.

For more information on setting up your practice, access the Young Physicians Publications List (AMA-YPS) through the AMA Web site at **www.ama-assn.org**. AMA members can access publications from this Web site that give information on board certification, preparation of a curriculum vitae, job search tips, what you need to know about contracts, resources for entering practice, and managed care.

Key Points

- Apply for a state medical license.
- Determine a target date for opening office.
- Decide where to locate your office.
- Determine what office supplies and equipment you will need.
- Develop administrative forms; check into computer systems and office software.
- Apply for hospital privileges.
- Contact health care plans to become a provider.
- Secure a business license.
- Reserve your office phone numbers.
- Develop a business plan; apply for a business loan.
- Secure malpractice insurance.
- Secure your office space; buy or rent office furniture.
- Hire an office manager; develop job descriptions; develop a filing system.
- Meet with your accountant and set up an accounting system.
- Develop a fee schedule.
- Secure a scheduling service, arrange for an answering service, a billing service, and a pager service.
- Develop a scheduling system.
- Develop a compliance plan.
- Order supplies and equipment.
- Hire other necessary personnel; find a temp service.
- Give notice of your practice opening.
- Start scheduling patients.
- Arrange for call sharing.
- Find a collection agency.
- Begin seeing patients.
- Advertise your practice.

ENDNOTES

1. See the AMA Web site at www.ama-assn.org/ama/pub/category/2644.html for the basics on getting a license and for links to state medical boards.
2. Contact www.nbme.org to download a request for certification of your passing the National Board of Medical Examiners (NBME) exam and for information on where to send the form for regular delivery or for overnight delivery. You can also write to the National Board of Medical Examiners, 3930 Chestnut Street, Philadelphia, Pennsylvania 19104, for certification of your passing the exam.
3. If you took the Federation Licensing Examination (FLEX), contact the Federation of State Medical Boards of the United States at www.fsmb.org or by writing to the Federation of State Medical Boards at 2626 B West Freeway, Fort Worth, Texas 76102 (817) 335-1141, for verification that you passed the examination. You can use their Federation Credentials Verification Service to

establish a confidential repository of your credentials that can be forwarded at your request to any interested party, including state medical boards, hospitals, managed care plans, and professional societies.
4. Contact the Educational Commission for Foreign Medical Graduates at www.ecfmg.org for certification verification service.
5. Obtain the DEA application from the Department of Justice, Drug Enforcement Administration, Registration Section, POB 28083, Central Station, Washington, D.C. 20005, (202) 633-1249. For information on obtaining or renewing a DEA license, you can also go to the Web site, www.deadiversion.usdoj.gov/drugreg/process.htm. The DEA homepage can be found at www.usdoj.gov/dea.
6. For example, "See patient information sheet dated [DATE], past medical, family, and social history."
7. Available at www.hcfa.gov/forms.
8. www.hcfa.gov/medicare/medicare.htm.
9. See www.hcfa.gov/medicaid/medicaid.htm for information about Medicaid. See medicaid.aphsa.org/members.htm for a list of state Medicaid directors and addresses.
10. www.bluecares.com.
11. See www.irs.gov to obtain an EIN and for tax information for small businesses.
12. See the IRS Web site at www.irs.ustreas.gov/bus_info and the Small Business Association Web site at www.sba.gov/starting for information about starting and operating a new small business, including whether your state requires a business license.
13. See the IRS Web site at www.irs.ustreas.gov/bus_info and the Small Business Association Web site at www.irs.ustreas.gov/bus_info for information about starting and operating a new small business.
14. Your city hall can give you information on obtaining a business license.
15. See the AMA Web site at www.ama-assn.org for ordering a CPT codebook.
16. See the AMA Web site at www.ama-assn.org for ordering an ICD codebook. Information is also available about ICD at www.cdc.gov/nchs/icd9.htm.

CHAPTER **6**

Your Office Equipment and Furnishings

It is exciting to set up your office and decorate your waiting room exactly as you like. Consider what arrangements will make your office most efficient and comfortable for your patients.

Your waiting room gives an impression of your practice. It should be cheerful and reflect your consideration for the patient's comfort. Light coming into the waiting room is cheerful and makes patients happy unless they are sitting by a window and visible to those outside. No one wants to be on display while waiting in a doctor's office, so make sure that there is light, but that no patient is exposed to the outside world. Soft, overstuffed upholstered furniture may be wonderful to sink into, but your elderly patients will have difficulty rising. You will want your furniture to be comfortable, but firm enough for a patient to rise as easily as possible. Armchairs are best, with firm bottoms of good quality leather. You will need furniture that can be easily wiped down in order to keep it clean. Your office furniture should be of excellent quality, but you do not want to give the impression that you have spent exorbitant amounts of money on the furnishings. If you treat children or anticipate that many patients will bring their children along, consider a small room with a television, VCR, and toys adjacent to the main waiting area.

The reception area should have a good view of the patient waiting room, as well as a view of the hall in the patient exam area. The reception window facing the waiting room should be separate from the patient check-out window in the exam room hall to prevent traffic jams as patients check in at one window and check out at the other. A door that can be closed should separate the waiting area from the exam room hallway. It is also helpful if the reception area is large enough to accommodate the file cabinets housing the patient charts, as well as the fax, copier, and other general office equipment.

Your file cabinets should be fire resistant and should provide a secure area for patient charts. Medical records must be kept private and may be released to someone other than the patient only with that patient's written request, which is signed by the patient and kept on record. You should have office forms specifically for requests for record transfers, with a blank to designate to whom the records should be sent and a blank for the patient's signature. You should have another form for a patient's signature when you request the patient's records from another office. Patient charts can be filed alphabetically or by number, and a color-coded system should be used to spot charts that are out of place.

You should have a separate billing office near the reception office. The billing office should have a door that can be closed and an extra chair for patients who need to have an extended discussion about their bill. In this office your staff member responsible for the billing can call insurance companies to follow up on collections; it is uncomfortable to have such conversations drifting out into the waiting area. The billing office should have a desk, a supply of insurance forms to bill any insurance companies who prefer paper billing, a computer for billing Medicare, Medicaid, and other insurance companies that accept electronic billing, and a file of contact names and phone numbers for each insurance company. Don't forget to buy a petty cash box or office safe.

Many different companies offer medical billing software. Talk with other physicians in your specialty to determine what medical billing software they use and if they are happy with the software. Call the software companies to discuss their products, and visit the Medisoft Web site,[1] as well as other medical billing sites for an idea of what medical billing software can do. Good billing software will store information for billing all types of health insurance, provide procedure and diagnosis codes, print Medicare forms if necessary, make billing payment status reports, include electronic claim submission capabilities, track numbers of patient visits, schedule appointments, and formulate reports, claims, and statements. The software companies should provide training seminars, as well as online help. Be sure to obtain backup software and equipment for your computer. Your computer hard drive should be backed up every night to prevent loss of data.

It is wise to outfit at least two exam rooms initially and expand as the patient load increases. While you are seeing a patient in one room, the medical assistant can escort a second patient into the other exam room, speak with the patient and document in the chart the patient's chief complaint—as well as any new information relevant to patient history or review of systems—and prepare the patient for your exam. To keep this sequence of events consistent, efficient, and comfortable for your patients, you will want a written office policy detailing exactly what you expect from your medical assistant. Chart holders mounted on the outside of the exam room door are helpful. There should be a supply cabinet for things that you need most often, roll paper for covering the exam table, and cleansing solution (from the medical supply catalogs) for wiping down tabletops. You will need a pillow handy, and an exam table. A mirror in the exam room is also very useful for the patient while getting dressed after the exam. Carpets are nice in the waiting areas and halls, but exam room floors should be carpet-free for easy cleaning. Remember to order patient gowns. Paper gowns will do, but if you prefer cloth gowns, you will need a laundry pick-up service.

Exam rooms should have a stool or chair for you, as well as another chair. The patient may prefer to wait for you in the chair rather than upon the exam table. Often there is a relative or a parent accompanying the patient, and it is important to make those waiting in the exam room as comfortable as possible. The patient and relative will be in a much better mood if the relative has not had to wait standing. Obviously there is a limit to the number of persons waiting in the exam rooms. Ask that only one person accompany the patient if many family members want to come along. The rest can wait in the waiting room. There should be a stool or chair for you to sit on for extended discussions, as well as a counter top or desk for you to use for your chart documentation. Make sure that the exam room is well lit and that the appropriate exam equipment is in every room that you use. You will need a sink in each exam room, a storage cabinet, and a trash container that complies with OSHA standards for disposal of blood products (see your medical supply catalog).

It is good to have a procedure room separate from your exam rooms. The procedure room should have a table that can be raised or lowered and should have good lighting. The procedure room can also be a good holding room for any patients who might feel faint. It should be wheelchair accessible for the handicapped.

Consider leasing your office telephones, your copier, and your computer system. Also consider leasing your expensive specialty equipment, such as x-ray machines or lasers. If you do decide to lease, be certain that there is an option to buy at the end of the lease. Also make sure that the lease specifies who is responsible for maintenance and repairs of the equipment. Some leases now require a percentage of the income from each procedure performed with the equipment. Have your attorney and accountant carefully review the lease agreement prior to signing it. Your accountant can counsel you about investment tax credits available for purchases of new business equipment versus tax deductions for leases. If you purchase equipment, consider purchasing a maintenance agreement. Make sure that the agreement provides for timely repair or replacement. You will not have time to deal with equipment that is not working.

Make sure that you have at least two toilets, one for patients near the exam rooms and the other near the back of the office for you and your staff. There should be facial tissues, plenty of paper towels, and spare toilet paper available so that the day is not interrupted to retrieve more supplies. Make sure that your patient restroom is handicap accessible.

If you have a laboratory for testing, you will need to contact CLIA for a license and for details regarding regulations for the laboratory. You will need a refrigerator for specimens separate from the refrigerator where you plan to keep food. The specimen refrigerator will need a thermometer to check adequate temperature. You will also need a sink for "clean jobs" that is separate from the sink where you wash instruments. You will need an autoclave and an area for packaging and autoclaving the instruments. You must periodically test the autoclave to make certain that it is functioning properly. Don't forget to have an appropriate fire extinguisher for your office. Check with your medical supply company to be sure that the extinguisher is appropriate for medical office fire protection. Have emergency phone numbers readily accessible and install smoke, fire, and burglary alarms in your office.

An adequate storage area is very important. If you plan to dispense samples provided by pharmaceutical representatives, be sure to determine your state regulations regarding drug samples. Likewise, if you plan to dispense other medications, check on your state regulations. Your state medical society and/or your state delegate to the American Medical Society will be an important source of information in this regard.

You will want to keep some of your medical specialty books handy, so plan to have a bookcase in your office. For the business office you will need a current CPT codebook, an ICD book, books that Medicare, Medicaid, and Blue Cross will send you once you become a provider, and a zip code book.

Don't forget products and procedures necessary to comply with OSHA. These include sharps containers, collection trays for used instruments, labels, gowns, masks, goggles, biohazard containers, red plastic liners for trash containers, eye wash attachments for your bathroom faucet, and other materials. Contact OSHA for a detailed list or buy an OSHA kit from either a supply catalog or the AMA.

You should consider installing several lines for your office telephone system. You will need at least two lines for incoming patient calls for appointments, inquiries, and problems. You will need a dedicated line for the insurance clerk to follow up on collections. You will want a private line for your office. Never scrimp and have too few phone lines. Your ability to get new patients will depend greatly on whether they can reach your office to make an appointment. Be sure that you have voice mail so that if someone cannot get through, he or she can leave a message. Be sure to return calls as quickly as possible.

Your office should be located toward the back so that regular patient traffic will not pass by your door as you make phone calls and attend to matters. You don't want a patient poised in the doorway waiting to talk with you during those private times.

Remember to plan for safety in case of fire. Have an evacuation plan in place and in writing in your policy manual. Make certain that all employees understand the policy.

Installation of a music system and subscription to a music service is an option to consider. Or you may want to avoid subscription charges and install a sound system that plays a series of CDs.

Key Points

- Your waiting room gives an impression of your practice.
- File cabinets should be fire resistant.
- Have a written office policy detailing what you expect your medical assistant to do.
- Consider leasing your equipment.
- Secure a CLIA license; develop an OSHA plan.
- Make an evacuation plan in case of fire.

ENDNOTE

1. medisoft4win@msoft.pair.com.

CHAPTER 7

Employees

Good employees can make or break an office. Place newspaper advertisements and look in the want ad section for employees advertising their skills and seeking employment. Obtain a post office box where applications can be sent. Contact the personnel office of local hospitals, and call local vocational or technical schools in the area for prospects.

As suggested in Chapter 4, hire an office manager on an hourly basis to help start your office. Let your office manager place the ads, seek candidates for the office staff, and bring a few of the best choices to you to interview. Continue the policy of involving office staff in decisions about hiring. As your staff grows, they should be involved in the interview and selection process. They will be more enthusiastic about new staff if they have been involved in the selection process. Be sure to check references of potential employees. If you are unable to reach the references given, ask for additional references. You will especially want to contact all previous employers.

How much should you pay an employee? Check with other offices in the area as well as with your accountant. You do not want to train and then lose an employee to a better paying job in another physician's office once the employee has gained experience working in a medical office. Do not be lulled by hopes of staff loyalty as you build up your office, promising to pay more in salaries down the road. Your staff members have financial needs and their training in your office makes them better candidates for securing better paying jobs. You can save money by paying an hourly rate to your employees at first, building the hours that you need them to work, but be sure to pay a reasonable rate. You may not want to offer benefits until your office grows and your staff is full-time and salaried. There are various benefit packages; your

45

accountant can advise you regarding which package is reasonable for your office.

Expect all staff members to be capable of performing all office functions so that if one member is out, another can cover for that member. Some offices require staff to rotate functions on a regular basis so that their skills for each office function are maintained. Whether you choose to do this or not, make clear to each staff member as he or she is hired that you expect not only performance of primary duties, but coverage if a co-worker is absent. Also make clear the working office hours, your expectations for Saturday coverage if any, and your policies regarding holidays, vacation, sick leave, and emergency leave. Explain benefits, give your new employee a copy of your office policy manual to read, and discuss how often staff members are paid. Indicate that all employees are hired for an initial probation period (usually three to six months).

Remember to train all office staff in use of emergency equipment and in office protocol regarding calls by patients, by physicians, and by others. Make certain that all office staff understand what procedures you perform and certain basic aspects of your practice so that they can respond intelligently to routine calls by patients. Most important, the staff should know what not to discuss with a caller and what to refer to you, the physician.

You should offer your staff the opportunity for training in Basic Life Support (BLS),[1] and in some cases Advanced Cardiac Life Support training (ACLS)[2] should be offered. Your local hospitals will have information regarding courses offered.

Remember to train your employees about OSHA requirements and to offer hepatitis vaccinations to each staff member. Your employees will be involved in preparing exam tables for each patient, in cleaning and autoclaving instruments, in transporting specimens to the collection boxes, and in many other activities directly relevant to OSHA requirements.

There are correspondence courses available on the Internet for training staff, including courses on OSHA and CLIA regulations, on medical terminology, billing, and other office functions. Investigate the availability of these courses if your staff needs further training or updating.[3]

Keep track of the office hours that each staff member works. This is important not only for your records but also to make sure that you are not violating minimum wage and overtime laws. Don't be lulled into feeling that your office is small and administrative matters can be kept informal. You will avoid misunderstandings among staff members if your policies are clear, fair, and understood by your staff from the beginning.

As your practice increases you may discover that your employees are scheduling according to their own preferences instead of for the benefit of the practice. You may find that you have seen the last patient earlier than expected, and yet discover that patients are being told the schedule is full. Even the most loyal of office staff can rationalize light scheduling. You should establish a routine of checking your schedule with your staff and giving advice as necessary about adding to or changing the schedule. Establish this custom from the beginning. At the end of the day, review your no-shows and cancellations and tell your staff what follow-up is needed for these patients. Ask your staff to update you on their follow-up.

One way to encourage efficient scheduling is to include in the salaries of your staff a percentage of your practice income. This incentive pay, even if based on a small percentage, can work wonders in creating an efficient office, keeping a full schedule of patients, stimulating effective billing and collections, and boosting morale.

Another problem that some physicians discover is that their receptionist, who always appears pleasant to them, is not always pleasant on the phone to patients who call. Periodically survey your patients to determine whether they are satisfied with their office visit and their treatment by you and your office staff. You can do this by talking with patients or by giving patient evaluation forms to patients at the beginning of their visit and asking them to turn in the forms after the visit. Review the evaluations and give feedback to your staff so that you can address criticisms and accommodate constructive recommendations. Small adjustments in how you or your staff members interact with patients can often make big differences.

For many years it was common to hear a medical practitioner say that he or she would only see patients and leave running the business part of the office to the staff. Many practitioners were shocked to discover that their office was not being run as they believed. In some instances, the well-trusted office manager had long been siphoning money from the practice. In other instances, billing and collections were inefficient or completely neglected, and patients not yet billed were turned over to collection agencies. Checks and balances within an office are extremely important to avoid these practices and should be in place from the start. Your accountant will advise you how to initiate these checks and balances. Most important, you should take part in the management of your office. Setting up an efficient system will require your attention to matters, but you will still have plenty of time to practice medicine. Avoid delegation of all business matters to your staff. You are a physician with a primary duty to patients, but you are also running a business, and you must view your practice accordingly. Expect loyalty, efficiency, and initiative, and show appreciation appropriately, but establish safeguards in your practice.

As you hire staff in the beginning and as you replace staff as necessary throughout your practice, you should be aware of the laws relevant to employee rights. The Fair Labor Standards Act[4] sets guidelines for minimum wages and overtime. Most employees[5] must be paid one and a half times their salary for hours worked in excess of 40 hours per week. For more information about the Fair Labor Standards Act, see the Department of Labor Web site[6] or write to the United States Department of Labor, Employee's Standards Administration, 200 Constitution Avenue, NW, Washington, D.C., 20210.

Your state may require you to contribute to an unemployment compensation fund based on your employee payroll and unemployment claims made by former employees. Your accountant will have this information, or you can check with your local medical society. An important aspect of requiring a probationary period for new employees is that if you decide to terminate the employee during the probationary period, you won't pay unemployment compensation to the employee.

EQUAL EMPLOYMENT OPPORTUNITY LAWS

It is unlawful to base your employment decisions upon race, color, religion, sex, or national origin.[7] Such decisions include hiring, firing, paying wages, determining promotions, providing training, and offering participation in retirement plans or other privileges of employment. You cannot refuse to give a staff member time off for observation of religious activities. It is unlawful to discriminate between employees on the basis of sex regarding payment of wages for substantially equal work.[8] It is unlawful to discriminate against your employees with respect to age[9] or with respect to physical disabilities that do not affect the job for which the individual is applying or hired.[10] The Civil Rights Act of 1991[11] provides for monetary damages in cases of intentional employment discrimination. Retaliation against an employee for filing a discrimination charge is prohibited. The Equal Employment Opportunity Commission (EEOC)[12] provides oversight and enforces these laws. Employers must post notices in places accessible to all employees advising them of their rights under the equal employment opportunity laws and informing them that they have a right to be free from retaliation for filing charges of discrimination.

It is important to understand these laws. For more information see the Equal Employment Opportunity Commission Web site at www.eeoc.gov/laws.

Key Points

- Expect all staff members to be capable of performing all office functions.
- Train your staff in use of emergency equipment and in office protocol.
- Train your employees in OSHA requirements.
- Offer hepatitis vaccinations.
- Be aware of minimum wage and overtime laws.
- Periodically monitor scheduling practices and staff interactions with patients.
- Survey patients for satisfaction with your office.
- Take part in the management of your office.
- Be aware of Equal Employment Opportunity Laws.

ENDNOTES

1. For information on BLS/CPR and for courses near you, contact www.cpr-ecc.org.
2. For information on ACLS and for practicing algorithms, see www.acls.net. To find a course in Advanced Cardiac Life Support (ACLS), Basic Life Support (BLS), or Pediatric Advanced Life Support (PALS) near you, contact www.proeducation.com/ecc/T_courses/Tcor_ACLS.htm or your local hospital.
3. Available, for example, at www.baker.edu/catalog/new/med.html.
4. 29 USCA §201, et seq.

5. This may not apply to certain executive, administrative, and professional employees. See the Department of Labor Web site at www.dol.gov for more information.
6. See the Department of Labor Web site at www.dol.gov.
7. The 1964 Civil Rights Act 42 USC §2000e (197w). Available at www.eeoc.gov/laws.html.
8. Equal Pay Act of 1963 (EPA) 29 USC §206(d). Available at www.eeoc.gov/laws.html.
9. Age Discrimination in Employment Act of 1967 (ADEA). 29 USC §621 (1967). The ADEA protects individuals who are 40 years of age or older from employment discrimination. Available at www.eeoc.gov/laws.html.
10. The American with Disabilities Act of 1990 (ADA) 42 USC §12101 (1977). Available at www.eeoc.gov/laws.html.
11. Civil Rights Act of 1991 Pub L No. 102-166. Available at www.eeoc.gov/laws.html.
12. See the Web site of the U.S. Equal Employment Opportunity Commission (EEOC) at www.eeoc.gov, or write to the U.S. Equal Employment Opportunity Commission (EEOC) Publications Distribution Center, P.O. Box 12549, Cincinnati, Ohio 45212-0549, for further information.

CHAPTER 8

Managed Care Contracts, Blue Cross/Blue Shield, Medicare, and Medicaid

Gone are the days when you set up shop, see patients, and collect money for the visit without further ado. Managed care is now an enormous presence in medical care. There are Health Maintenance Organizations (HMOs), Preferred Provider Organizations (PPOs), Physician Hospital Organizations (PHOs), Point of Service Organizations (POSs), and others. HMOs provide health care services for their beneficiaries, who pay a fixed monthly amount. HMOs place emphasis on control of health care costs. Referrals are usually required from a primary care physician ("gatekeeper") for a patient to see a specialist. PPOs provide fee-for-service health care services at a discount and usually do not require a gatekeeper. POSs usually require a gatekeeper, but if the patient wants to see a specialist and not go through the gatekeeper, the patient can do so by paying a penalty fee. PHOs are organizations of physicians and hospitals that impart strength in numbers in negotiating with managed care organizations regarding provision of care to the organizations.

In many areas where a large percentage of the population belongs to managed care groups, it is vital for a physician to sign up as a provider with these groups in order to survive financially. Sometimes there is no problem in signing up. Just call the managed care group, indicate that you would like to be a provider; they will send you the forms to review and sign, and you are in. Some managed care groups may be closed to further membership, and you will be blocked from them until they open.

It is very important to determine what managed care groups are important in your area and to discuss with the physicians in the area what problems and benefits they have found with the different groups. There are a number of different types of such groups. Some are physician-owned; others are not. As mentioned, some require primary physician gatekeepers who refer patients to specialists when the gatekeepers decide that this is necessary. Many managed care groups have risk sharing, where a portion of the provider's payment is withheld for the fiscal year until it is determined whether the provider has kept expenses within a budgeted amount. If so, he can receive all or a portion of the withheld amount; if not, he forfeits all or a portion.

The managed care group will send to the provider physician updates of its schedule of reimbursement for services rendered to the patients enrolled in the managed care group. It is important to make sure that you have the most updated schedule for billing. By signing up with the managed care group, the physician usually agrees to adhere to the schedule.

When applying to become a provider with a managed care group, you will usually be asked to send in a great deal of information. This can become extremely tedious when you are applying to many managed care groups. Keep your credentials file handy in your office to photocopy for each application. You'll need copies of your curriculum vitae as well as copies of up-to-date licenses (e.g., State Medical License, State Controlled Substances License, DEA License) to send with each application. You will need details of any malpractice action pending or active against you. You'll often need a timetable explaining what you have done from medical school on—keep this list handy so that you don't have to reconstruct it over and over again.

Whether you are in solo practice or in a group, you will need to fill out these applications to become a provider for managed care groups. It is important, therefore, to be aware of some of the contractual provisions that you may find and the obligations that they impose. You may want your office staff to fill out the standard information on the applications, such as name, office address, Medicare and Medicaid numbers, DEA numbers, hospitals where you have privileges, and so on, and to attach copies of your license documents. But read over whatever has been filled in on your behalf. Your signature acknowledges that you agree with everything within, so be sure that you do agree.

Managed care contracts may have restrictions that would create conflicts for you regarding patient care, and you should read them carefully and should have an attorney review them. "Gag rules" are sometimes found in these contracts that may prevent you from discussing options with patients. There may be restrictions on patient referral and transfer that would inhibit your ability to give the quality of care that you expect to give and that your patients expect to receive. These applications that require your signature become a contract with legal duties, and ignoring the provisions can result in breach of contract.

Have an attorney review managed care contracts to revise language with which you do not agree. In some cases the managed care organizations will hold firm and not allow changes. But do not sign the contracts unless you feel comfortable doing so. Discuss your discomfort about certain provisions with the managed care organization. Discuss with your attorney your concerns and listen to his or her advice.

The AMA Web site[1] contains a model managed care health services agreement with comments about what to watch out for in a managed care agreement.

BLUE CROSS AND BLUE SHIELD

The Blue Cross and Blue Shield[2] system is the oldest and largest health care insurer in the United States and is comprised of forty-eight independent, locally operated Blue Cross and Blue Shield member plans. Originally, Blue Cross plans covered hospital care and Blue Shield plans covered physicians' services, but now most Blue Cross and Blue Shield plans are single corporations or at least work closely together. More than eighty percent of hospitals across the United States contract with Blue Cross and Blue Shield plans.

Blue Cross and Blue Shield plans offer different types of Medicare coverage including "Medigap" policies and Medicare-qualified HMOs. By signing up with Blue Cross, you agree to provide services to Blue Cross subscribers and to accept payment according to the Blue Cross payment plan. Some plans allow the physician to bill to the patient the balance of the physician charges. Other plans require acceptance as full fee the amount that Blue Cross pays for services to the patient. Because Blue Cross usually has a large number of subscribers in any given area, you will probably want to sign up with Blue Cross as a provider very early during the process of setting up an office. Review the plan options carefully with your accountant to determine which plans you want to participate in as a subscriber.

MEDICARE AND MEDICAID

Medicare

Medicare[3] is a federal health insurance program for people 65 years or older, people who are disabled, and people with permanent kidney failure. Medicare Part A provides coverage of inpatient hospital services, skilled nursing facilities, home health services, and hospice care. Medicare Part B helps pay for costs of physician services, outpatient hospital services, and medical equipment and supplies. Sometimes referred to as Part C, the Medicare+Choice program[4] expands beneficiary options for participating in various private-sector health care plans.

Medicare does not cover some health care services such as long-term nursing care and dental care, some medical appliances such as dentures, eyeglasses, and hearing aids, and most prescription drugs. However, some Medicare health plans, including Medigap,[5] may provide coverage in some of these areas. Medigap plans are private health insurance policies that cover some of the medical costs that Medicare does not cover.

Fee-for-service beneficiaries are responsible for charges not covered by Medicare unless the beneficiary has other coverage that will pay. Beneficiaries enrolled in Medicare+Choice plans share in payment based on the specific plan chosen.

Payments to hospitals are made under the prospective payment system (PPS), where a specific amount, based on diagnosis-related group (DRG) classification, is paid for each in-patient hospital stay.

Physicians are paid based on the lesser of either the submitted charge or an amount determined by a relative value scale (RVS). You must decide whether you want to "take assignment" with Medicare or not. If you take assignment, you must consider payments made to you by Medicare for a patient's care as full payment for that service. You cannot request any additional payment for that service from the patient or from Medicare. You can, however, collect deductibles and co-insurance, as well as payment for any services not covered by Medicare. You must not bill Medicare for services not medically necessary. Medicare considers billing of medically unnecessary services fraudulent.

Medicare (part B) pays eighty percent of the allowable charge, and the patient pays twenty percent. Before Medicare payment occurs, however, the patient must have met his or her annual deductible. Be sure that your office staff calls Medicare to determine whether the patient has met the deductible. If not, you will need to collect from the patient.

If you do not take assignment, the patient can be charged for the excess that you bill over and above what Medicare will pay. Medigap insurance will sometimes pay this excess. There are now limits on the excess amount that physicians can charge Medicare beneficiaries.

Peer review organizations (PROs) are groups of physicians or other health care professionals who oversee the care provided to Medicare beneficiaries in each State. The Department of Health and Human Services (HHS) oversees the Medicare program, with most administrative responsibility falling within the Health Care Financing Administration (HCFA) of HHS.

For more information about Medicare contact www.medicare.gov.

Medicaid

Medicaid,[6] funded cooperatively by both federal and by state governments, pays for medical assistance for low-income persons and families if they fall within certain "medically needy" categories. Each state, within federal guidelines, sets its own eligibility criteria for enrollment in Medicaid, determines the scope of coverage, and establishes the rate and method of payment for certain services.

Providers who participate in Medicaid must accept whatever Medicaid pays as payment in full.

Medicare beneficiaries with low incomes may also be eligible for Medicaid. There may be coverage for prescription drugs, eyeglasses, and hearing aids.

Key Points

- Maintain a credentials file.
- Examine managed care contracts carefully.
- Sign up with Blue Cross/Blue Shield, Medicare, and Medicaid.
- Medicare does not cover some health care services.
- You must bill Medicare only for medically necessary services.
- Providers that participate in Medicaid must accept what Medicaid pays as payment in full.

ENDNOTES

1. Available at www.ama-assn.org.
2. Available at www.bluecares.com.
3. Available at www.hcfa.gov/medicare/medicare.htm.
4. Information available at www.medicare.gov/Choices/Overview.asp.
5. Information available at www.medicare.gov/Choices/Overview.asp.
6. Available at www.hcfa.gov/medicaid.

CHAPTER 9

Coding

HISTORY, EXAM, AND MEDICAL DECISION MAKING

Billing Medicare or Medicaid[1] carries certain obligations. If HCFA[2] audits your charts, HCFA will look for documentation of certain elements of a patient visit to determine whether the correct level of service has been billed. These elements are chief complaint, history of present illness, patient history (prior medical, social, and family history), review of systems, exam, and medical decision making. The nature of the presenting problems, extent of history, review of systems, exam, and medical decision making determine what evaluation and management (E/M) level is appropriate in billing for a patient visit.

In billing for a patient visit, first categorize the patient as a "new patient" or an "established patient." A new patient has had no services rendered during the past three years by you or by others of your specialty within your group practice. An established patient has received professional services from you or from another of your specialty within your group practice within the past three years.

Your documentation must reflect all of the necessary elements relevant to the level of E/M service or procedure billed, and your documented diagnoses must be consistent with the diagnosis codes used. Every office visit billed requires documentation of a chief complaint. This is often documented in the patient's words.

Medicare requires documentation of history, exam, and medical decision making for each new patient for which a bill is submitted. For established patients, only two of these three elements are required. For each new patient you should document past medical history, family history, social history, history of the present

57

problem, review of systems, exam, and medical decision making. Past medical history, family history, social history, and review of systems can be obtained from a well-designed new patient information form that is filled out by each new patient. To get credit for documenting these elements at each return patient visit, you will not need to re-document the specific information if you indicate that you have reviewed this form and have documented any changes in the information since the last visit.

Current guidelines can be found on the AMA Web site[3] and the HCFA Web site[4] that detail the extent of history, exam, and medical decision making necessary for billing the different E/M levels. The guidelines are subject to change, so be sure to read the bulletins sent out by the Health Care Financing Association (HCFA) and to periodically check the AMA Web site for the most current version. CPT and ICD codebooks change annually, so keep the most recent version in your office. Contact your specialty association for more details about coding for your specific specialty.

At the time of printing, a new patient visit is coded as 99201, 99202, 99203, 99204, or 99205 depending upon the complexity of the history, the exam, and the medical decision making. Refer to your coding book or the AMA Web site to determine the current criteria for establishing the complexity of these elements. An established patient visit can be coded as 99211, 99212, 99213, 99214, or 99215, again depending upon the complexity of the history, the exam, and the medical decision making. An office consult is likewise billed as 99241, 99242, 99243, 99244, or 99245. There are also codes for hospital consultations.

A consult (consultation) is a professional evaluation of a patient at the request of another physician. Medicare and other providers usually reimburse a consult at a higher rate than a regular office visit. If you bill for a consult, however, you must be sure that the visit fits the definition of a consult, you must document a request from another physician for a consultation, and you must document that you have sent a report back to the requesting physician. There is an expectation that a report will be sent back to the requesting physician. The fact that a procedure may also be rendered does not invalidate categorizing the service as a consult. You should keep a copy in the patient's chart of your report back to the requesting physician. The Medicare claim for the consult visit must include the UPIN[5] of the requesting physician. A consult is distinguished from a referral, which is billed as a regular office visit, in that a referral constitutes simply a physician referral of a patient to another physician for care. Although no reply to the referring physician is necessary for billing purposes regarding a referral, it is nevertheless courteous and good business practice to send a letter to the referring physician expressing appreciation for the referral and describing your evaluation and treatment plan for the patient.

The patient visit codes are called evaluation and management (E/M) codes. There are also codes for procedures. All of these codes are found in a CPT codebook. Each E/M code and procedure code billed must be accompanied by a diagnosis code. Diagnosis codes are found in the ICD codebook. The codebooks can be ordered from medical book suppliers, through your specialty association, or through the AMA.

For a particular patient visit, you can bill only one E/M code. If the patient has a second problem that requires a procedure, then you can bill both for the E/M for the first problem and for the procedure related to the second problem. In this case, you would add a 25 modifier to the E/M code (e.g., 99213-25) to signify that the E/M billing is for a separate problem from the procedure that you are also billing. You can bill more than one procedure code if more than one procedure is performed. If you perform multiple procedures, add a 59 modifier to all except the first procedure to indicate that the procedures are distinct or independent from other services performed on the same day.

A global period attaches to certain procedures. Medicare considers that the cost of the follow-up care for a procedure conducted during the "global period" for that procedure is included in the amount that Medicare pays you for the procedure itself. If the patient comes back to you with a problem unrelated to the procedure but the global period for the procedure is still in effect, Medicare will assume that the separate problem is related to the procedure and payment will be rejected. In order to be paid for evaluation of this separate problem, you must use a modifier 24 with the E/M code to indicate that you are seeing the patient for a problem unrelated to the procedure. See your specialty codebook to determine global periods for procedures that you conduct.

CODING

A modifier 57 used with an E/M code indicates that your E/M service has resulted in an initial decision to perform surgery on the same day as the E/M service and allows you to bill for both an E/M and a procedure with the same diagnosis code. Use modifier 58 when you perform a staged or related procedure or service during the postoperative period, such as a re-excision. Use modifier 76 for a repeat procedure by the same physician. Modifier 79 designates an unrelated procedure or service during the postoperative period. Codes as well as guidelines change. See your up-to-date coding manual for further descriptions, to update changes, and to see examples relevant to your specialty.[6]

Be sure to contact your local Medicare representative when you set up your office to obtain a booklet about Medicare. Read thoroughly both the booklet and the periodic updates that will be sent to you. You and your staff should be familiar with coding, submitting claims, understanding why claims are rejected, how those rejected can be resubmitted, and how appeals can be made. Deadlines can attach to these processes, so it is important that your staff proceed with timeliness and efficiency. Information on coding is also available at www.hcfa.gov/audience/planprov.htm, and information about general principles of medical record documentation is available at www.hcfa.gov/medicare/1995dg.pdf.

Key Points

- The nature of the presenting problems, the extent of history, review of systems, exam, and medical decision making determine the appropriate evaluation and management level in billing.
- Current coding guidelines are found on the AMA and HCFA Web sites.
- A consult is a professional evaluation of a patient at the request of another physician.

ENDNOTES

1. Other carriers are following suit in requiring documentation consistent with that required by HCFA.
2. Available at www.hcfa.gov.
3. Available at www.ama-assn.org.
4. Available at www.hcfa.gov/audience/planprov.htm.

5. A Unique Physician Identification Number (UPIN) will be sent to you when you sign up to be a Medicare provider. You must indicate your UPIN number when you bill Medicare. To determine the UPIN number of another physician in billing Medicare for a consult, you can contact the Government Printing Office at 202 512-1800 or your local part B Medicare carrier (see **www.hcfa.gov/ upin/UPINTOC.htm**) for a list.
6. Please note that these codes are in effect at the time of this printing, but you should check the AMA Web site to verify the current correct codes.

CHAPTER **10**

Running Your Office

Setting up a practice involves a lot of work, but you will have the satisfaction of knowing that it is your office, exactly as you created it. It can grow and take shape as you continue to evolve into a better physician and a better director and owner of your office. Let's now look at some of the aspects of running the office that you set up. We will revisit some previous topics and we will cover others in greater depth.

A PATIENT SCHEDULES AN APPOINTMENT

A patient, Mrs. Brown, has called your office for an appointment. Your receptionist has been courteous and accommodating. A few questions have established that the patient is new to your office, that her problem can be addressed by your medical specialty, and that you are a provider for her insurance plan. Your receptionist has answered Mrs. Brown's questions and has given her directions to your office, as well as other relevant information such as parking accommodations. Your receptionist has scheduled Mrs. Brown's appointment, and has mailed a patient information form to her to be completed and brought to the office at the time of the visit. Mrs. Brown has been asked to come fifteen minutes earlier than the scheduled appointment to complete other necessary paperwork. Let's now consider the flow of events from the time that she arrives at your office until she leaves.

THE PATIENT ARRIVES AT YOUR OFFICE

Mrs. Brown enters a pleasant waiting room with comfortable, sturdy chairs. She notes the magazines on the coffee tables or in the magazine rack, as well as the welcome brochure that you have placed in the waiting room. She is welcomed by the receptionist and asked to check in at the reception counter. The sign-in sheet will have space for name, time of appointment, and time of arrival. Mrs. Brown gives the completed patient information sheet to the receptionist. If Mrs. Brown has forgotten to bring the sheet, she is given another one and helped to complete it if necessary. The receptionist photocopies Mrs. Brown's insurance card. Mrs. Brown is asked to sign a form authorizing the release of medical or related information about Mrs. Brown to HCFA, or any other health care coverage entity, and of any information necessary for related health care claims. (This patient authorization form should be updated each year.) The receptionist also asks Mrs. Brown to sign an assignment of benefits form. The form authorizes release of information necessary for processing the claim and assigns insurance benefits, to which the patient is entitled, to the physician. This is relevant to Medicare billing if you are going to accept assignment, and to billing of non-Medicare entities. You may want your receptionist to make a copy of the driver's license of each new patient in case the patient wants to pay by check. The receptionist courteously asks Mrs. Brown to have a seat and tells her that the doctor will be with her shortly.

Mrs. Brown reads the welcome brochure, which tells her about your practice, including procedures that you perform, call coverage, answering service, prescription refill policies, payment at time of service policies, and numbers to call for appointments and for emergencies. The brochure also mentions your policy about payment of co-pays, deductibles, or non-covered services at the time of service. (You may also want a small sign at the check-out window stating that payment is requested at the time of service.)

Mrs. Brown's chart is prepared, including the patient information sheet that she has completed, a photocopy of her insurance card, the signed assignment of benefits form, and the signed form authorizing release of information necessary for processing insurance claims. On the inside cover—or in another easily accessible area— is an update list for problems and medications. This includes spaces for dates that medications are stopped and dates that you or any other physicians prescribe new medications. Allergies can also be indicated on the list or stamped on the front of the chart.

There should be a dated progress note page or pages and sections within the chart for lab reports, x-ray reports, consults, and other information relevant to treatment of the patient.

Mrs. Brown's chart is placed with previously pulled charts in order of appointment time for the day. Your medical assistant picks up Mrs. Brown's chart and courteously escorts her to an exam room. Your assistant reviews Mrs. Brown's patient information, including present medications and medical problems, and asks Mrs. Brown her reason for seeing the doctor today. The medical assistant records this information on the progress note along with vital signs and any other helpful information regarding Mrs. Brown's chief complaint. Mrs. Brown is given an examination gown, if appropriate, and your assistant tells Mrs. Brown that you will be in to see her in a few minutes. Your assistant indicates by exam room door flag that Mrs. Brown is to be seen first, and places Mrs. Brown's chart in the door chart holder.

Mr. Smith enters the waiting area. Mr. Smith is a returning patient. The receptionist greets Mr. Smith as he signs in. The receptionist verifies whether Mr. Smith's address, phone number, or insurance information has changed since his last visit, and if so, the receptionist makes the appropriate changes to your office records. (It is very important to have the patient's updated phone number to be able to call and remind patients of their appointment a day ahead of time, and in case you need to cancel appointments.) The receptionist courteously asks Mr. Smith to have a seat. Your assistant escorts Mr. Smith to an exam room and discusses with him any changes in medications or allergies. The assistant enters the patient's chief complaint as well as other complaints, current medications, allergies, vital signs, and other helpful information on the progress note and gives Mr. Smith an exam gown if appropriate to the problem(s) to be examined. The assistant indicates by exam room door flag that Mr. Smith is the second patient for you to see, and puts Mr. Smith's chart in the door chart holder.

You enter the exam room where Mrs. Brown is waiting and greet her. You discuss her problem and review with her the information that she has entered on the patient information form, now within her chart. This information should contain, in addition to the chief complaint, any medications, allergies, and her past medical,

RUNNING YOUR OFFICE   65

family, and social history. You note whether she has come to you at the request of another physician for consultation, whether she has been referred for treatment, or has come on her own. You then examine her with your assistant present, decide on a treatment plan, and proceed with your plan. You indicate when you would like her to return for follow-up and mark on the patient encounter form attached to Mrs. Brown's chart your billing codes for the visit (see Chapter 9 for information on coding). You dictate or write the progress note, either during or immediately following Mrs. Brown's visit. You have developed a system for dictating or writing progress notes that includes chief complaint(s), history of present illness, exam findings, assessment, and plan and that will allow you to retrieve information quickly. You use this system as you record Mrs. Brown's visit.

Remember that the medical chart is a legal document and that a patient can request a copy of the chart at any time, so never insert wry remarks, regardless of how tempting. If you are dictating, be sure to put enough notes in your chart so that if the patient calls or returns before the dictation is transcribed, you will know the reason for his or her visit and what you have prescribed. Indicate in the chart that you have dictated the note and sign it so that if your charts are audited, those charts with dictation not yet transcribed will indicate that your brief notes are not the entire note for the visit. Be sure to date and record all patient contacts whether an office visit, a call by or to a patient, or a call by another physician about the patient. If you write your notes, make sure that your handwriting is legible. If you are audited and the auditors can't read the note, you get no credit for documentation. If you are charging for a consultation, be sure to send a letter back to the consulting physician. If the visit is for a referral only, be sure to send a letter of thanks to the referring party.

Before you leave Mrs. Brown, you ask your assistant to follow up with her about what you have already discussed regarding the treatment plan and to answer any questions that Mrs. Brown may have.

This assumes that the assistant will give the standard answers that you have instructed to be given. Delegating appropriate duties to your assistant will allow you more time with patients for the things that only you can do. A capable assistant should be able to dress sites of surgical procedures, distribute and discuss printed information on wound care with patients, give general health care information, and discuss care relevant to the patient's clinical problems. Make clear to your assistant which counseling is appropriate and what to say. Make sure that the staff member gives the patient the printed information after discussing the information with the patient. Be available for any questions that cannot be answered by the assistant. Good interactions between the assistant and the patient will help the patient feel that his or her problems have been carefully heard and attended to. Remember, however, that you are responsible for the actions of your assistant in matters that you delegate to him or her in your office. Make sure that your assistant is well trained and competent to do the jobs consistent with your expectations.

You have now dictated your note and are going in to see Mr. Smith. Mrs. Brown is at the check-out window, and your receptionist notes the codes that you have listed on the patient encounter form. Your receptionist checks Mrs. Brown's insurance information and determines if she has met her deductible and/or if she owes a co-payment. Your receptionist also checks if any procedures were performed that were not covered by Mrs. Brown's insurance, and collects any amounts due from Mrs. Brown. Your receptionist schedules a follow-up appointment for Mrs. Brown and gives her an appointment card.

In the meantime, the medical assistant has put fresh paper on the exam table in the room vacated by Mrs. Brown, has wiped down appropriate surfaces in accordance with OSHA regulations, and has put the next patient in the exam room.

A word about chaperones: Always call in a chaperone when there is any doubt that a patient may be uncomfortable with an examination or procedure, or when the patient is a minor and there may be a chance of misinterpretation of your intent. For examination or procedures of the breast, genital, or anal areas, it is best to have a chaperone if possible. Provide adequate exam gowns and drapes so that the areas not examined can be kept covered. Remember that if your patient chooses to interpret wrongly your intent or your actions, you risk your reputation, license, and financial security, even if your manner was entirely professional. If you were alone with the patient, it is your word against the patient's claims. A chaperone can reassure the patient, lessening the likelihood of misinterpretations of your intentions, and serve as witness to your appropriate actions, lessening the likelihood that the patient will file frivolous charges. You should make certain that the patient understands what you plan to do and why it is necessary and that the patient consents to the examination or procedure.

BILLING

Your staff enters the codes billed and the amount paid by Mrs. Brown and either sends them electronically[1] or, using appropriate claims forms, prints a bill for the relevant insurance company. Your computer program will also allow your staff to schedule, assimilate patient information, and perform accounting functions. If you prefer, you can enter your progress notes at a computer terminal or use voice recognition technology to dictate your notes to the computer rather than using a handheld recorder or writing your notes.

If an insurance company does not accept electronic billing, the computer information can be transferred to the appropriate claim form and mailed. Medicare-printed claim forms are called HCFA 1500 forms and can be ordered from medical office supply companies. These standard HCFA forms are printed in a certain red ink that cannot be duplicated by computer. Many other insurance companies accept these forms also. Check with the insurance or managed care companies to determine what forms are required. Although you can download HCFA 1500 forms from the Internet and some software programs will print these forms[2] from the computer, only certain states will allow these office-computer printed or downloaded forms. States that require the standard forms and those that allow computer-printed forms are listed on the HCFA Web site.[3]

If you are using the pegboard system initially until you purchase your computer and office software system, the following would have occurred on the day of Mrs. Brown's visit. Upon arriving at the office in the morning, the receptionist would have entered the date at the top of a "day sheet," a large sheet of ruled paper with fee slips attached. A ledger card would have been prepared for Mrs. Brown's account upon her arrival in the office. When Mrs. Brown arrived at the check-out window after the patient visit, the receptionist would have entered charges and payments simultaneously on the fee slips, ledger card, and day sheet, using carbon paper. The receptionist would have given Mrs. Brown a copy of the fee slip as her receipt. At the end of the day, the charges and income for the day would be totaled, and the total from the previous day sheet would be brought forward to keep a running account of charges posted and income received. The ledger cards for the patients seen during the day would be replaced in the ledger card file, and photocopies of the ledger cards would be mailed to patients at billing time. The pegboard system is a workable solution if you need to keep expenses down when you first start your office. It can be replaced by a computer system and office software when possible, but remember that you then will need to enter all of the data that you have accumulated on the day sheets.

Collecting

Make sure that your staff vigorously tries to collect accounts receivables. Bills showing amounts still due after 60 days should include reminders that payment must be sent as soon as possible to avoid turning over the account to a collection agency. If your staff has tried to collect amounts owed more than six months but the amounts are still outstanding and no attempt has been made to arrange for payment, turn the accounts over to a collection service.

If the accounts are overdue because of a lack of response or a rejected claim from an insurance company, your staff should aggressively follow up with the insurance company. Time is of the essence in such matters since insurance companies or managed care organizations will no longer address payment matters after a certain period of time. Your signed agreement with the managed care organization likely will contain such language to avoid very late claims. The organization may refuse to pay, objecting that the wrong code was used or that more information needs to be sent or making any other argument, using up the time that you have to properly submit the claim. Delay in responding to the objection of the insurance company can therefore be fatal to your ability to collect. Your staff should be quick to follow up on such rejected or ignored claims. You may want to dedicate one business phone line to following up on claims with insurance companies since the companies will often put your staff on hold for long periods of time before answering, tying up office phone lines.

Assignment and Deductibles

Payment from Medicare for services that you have rendered to a Medicare patient comes to you if you have accepted assignment. If you have not accepted assignment, the payment goes to the patient, who is expected to then pay you. If you have accepted assignment, Medicare pays you eighty percent of your fee profile. Medicare establishes your fee profile based on your usual charge for services rendered. You may bill the patient for the remaining twenty percent of your fee profile. In the case of Medicaid, you must accept whatever Medicaid sends as payment in full. Medicare's payment is contingent upon the patient's having met his or her deductible. The deductible is a certain amount that the patient must pay up front each year for his or her health care before Medicare payments will start. Most patients will need to pay toward their deductible near the first of the year. Other insurances may also have a deductible. Be sure that your staff determines for each patient visit the patient's deductible and collects the appropriate amount from the patient for the patient visit.

Patients that belong to managed care organizations must usually make a co-payment at the time of the office visit. It is very important to determine this amount and to collect it from the patients at the time of the office visit. You should keep up-to-date health insurance information for all of your patients and have your staff call the insurance company for updates on a patient's deductible status.

SCHEDULING

Schedule more patients toward the beginning of the hour. In one flexible system, called "wave scheduling," a certain number of patients are booked during the same time interval during the first part of the hour and the latter part of the hour is left free. Having patients arrive in waves accommodates the variations in early, on time, or late arrival of patients and leaves time for catching up or working in emergencies or walk-ins. Determine the average length of an appointment, calculate how many patients per hour you can see based on the length of the average patient visit, and then schedule this number of patients to arrive at intervals within the first part of each hour, seeing each in order of his or her arrival. Schedule surgeries or other time-consuming procedures within dedicated time periods separate from your non-surgical patient visits. New patients will need additional time and should come in fifteen minutes earlier than their scheduled appointment. Avoid booking new patients at the end of the day if possible. Ask your staff to call each patient scheduled for the following day to remind the patient of the appointment.

RETURNING PHYSICIAN CALLS

Return physician calls promptly. Ask your staff to notify you if a physician is calling, and take the call immediately if possible. If the matter requires long discussion, you and the physician can make arrangements for a follow-up call later, but be sure to take the call initially.

RESPONDING TO REFERRALS OR REQUESTS FOR CONSULTS

Be sure to send a letter of appreciation to a physician who has referred a patient to you. Briefly describe the patient's condition and your treatment plan. Also dictate a letter to a physician requesting a consultation. Indicate the patient's condition, your treatment, and your recommendations for further treatment of the patient.

CASH ON HAND

You will need a small amount of cash for making change when patients pay their bill in cash. Put money in this fund by writing an office check and require your staff to keep careful records of any disbursement from this fund. The fund must not be used for any other purpose. In addition, have a separate petty cash fund for purchasing small items such as soft drinks or toilet tissue. Write an office check to put money into this fund and require your staff to keep receipts of any use of this fund. Keep both of these funds in a locked, secure place.

FINANCIAL REPORTS

You will need to have financial reports produced periodically to keep track of your accounts receivables, income, and collection rate. You will need to pay estimated income tax and will need to prepare quarterly tax returns. Discuss with your accountant what you need to do at first as your practice gets started and how you need to set up your office accounting to keep the appropriate records. The accountant can prepare tax returns, calculate estimated tax payments, set up payroll accounts, review the office accounting records, and periodically audit to make certain that the records are being adequately kept.

POLICIES

Develop policies for your office and put them in writing in a policy manual. Policies set a standard for your office staff in their duties and promote consistency and efficiency in running the office. Policies can be modified as necessary. Your staff should feel that they are a part of the policy making, with you making the final decisions.

Use your policy manual when training new employees. Your policies should address such matters as interactions with patients, office hours, time sheets, time off for vacation and for sickness, timing for consideration of pay raises, and periodic review of staff performance. Your policies should indicate that you expect the staff to attend and participate in office staff meetings. Provide for education in OSHA, CLIA, and other relevant federal regulations, including compliance with Medicare and Medicaid billing, and require your staff to uphold these regulations. Your policies should address the importance of hepatitis vaccination and the right of each staff member to have the vaccination.

Hire staff for a trial period and specify this policy within the manual. Address staff benefits. Discuss benefit packages and costs with companies that design such packages for employers.

The AMA has developed policies that relate to both ethical and legal issues and include issues such as professional courtesy, waiver of co-pay, patient confidentiality, informed consent, and termination of the patient/physician relationship. See the AMA Web site[4] for more details.

PATIENT SATISFACTION

Start the office day promptly; a patient will become upset if forced to wait for a long time in the waiting room without an explanation. Ask your staff to give your apologies if you are delayed, and repeat your apology when you see the patient in the exam room.

Periodically survey your patients about their satisfaction with your staff and with your treatment of them. Once every three or four months designate a day for your staff to give each patient an anonymous evaluation form to complete after their office visit. Carefully consider any constructive criticism, and take steps to correct matters as necessary. Your staff will be more conscious about having pleasant interactions with patients if they are aware of such periodic evaluations. Don't cancel appointment days often. Both your staff and your patients feel the effects of cancellations. If you need to cancel, have your staff give a brief explanation and apology to the patients and try to accommodate them as much as possible in rescheduling. Always schedule the patient as soon as possible if the problem is very worrisome to the patient. Remember that your patients are the best advertisement for your practice, and so it is important to understand and eliminate any reasonable dissatisfaction that they feel.

AT THE END OF THE DAY

You've seen your last patient and have returned calls to patients as necessary. Your staff has placed any specimens in the appropriate collection boxes for pickup by the appropriate labs. You have completed all dictation, and you have the office deposits to deposit in the bank. You have reviewed all cancelled appointments as well as no-shows, and you have asked the receptionist to call all no-shows and cancellations the following morning to determine whether the medical problems are still present and to reschedule as necessary. Be sure to tell your staff which patients must return. If your staff has made three attempts to reschedule but has not been able to reach a patient or the patient continues to cancel, send a registered letter stating the importance of follow-up treatment and keep a copy in the chart. Document a no-show or cancellation on the patient's chart, and date and sign it.

HOSPITAL ROUNDS

You may decide to make your hospital rounds early in the morning or at the end of your office day. Be sure to obtain all patient information necessary for billing (usually found on a patient information sheet at the beginning of the patient's hospital chart) and to bring back to your office a copy of your hospital progress note.

AFTER HOURS COVERAGE

You will likely want to share call with other local physicians in your specialty area. Discuss this when you initially meet with the other specialists in your community early in setting up your practice.

DRUG REPRESENTATIVES

Drug representatives will come to your office to share information about their products with you. You may feel that your interactions with the representatives take up time that you need for seeing patients, but the information that they give can be very helpful in keeping you up to date on the latest treatment products. The samples that the representatives leave will be much appreciated by your patients. You will, of course, need to evaluate the products yourself to determine whether they are as effective as promoted by the company. You will also need to keep an inventory of the samples and discard any that are out-of-date. State regulations vary as to the degree of labeling and other paperwork necessary for dispensing samples in a physician's office. Check with your state medical society for your state regulations.

OPENING MAIL

Decide who will open the mail, post the receipts, write checks for the office bills that you must pay, and post these payments. You should review and sign all checks, and you should review each day's receipts. Your office manager can make out the deposit slip for the receipts and enter the amounts in your records, but you should make the deposit in the bank night deposit box on your way home.

EMERGENCY EQUIPMENT AND PROTOCOL

Train your office staff in the use of emergency procedures and equipment in the office. Make provisions for periodic retraining and updating of emergency protocols. Make certain that your staff understands which calls should be considered emergencies and what instructions should be given to the patient regarding coming to the emergency room or to the office. Discuss with your staff when you should be notified immediately.

HANDLING CALLS

Instruct your staff on handling all types of calls, including emergencies, calls from physicians, calls from irate patients, business calls, calls from hospitals, and personal calls. Discuss with them the correct response to each type of call and what protocols should be followed for each type of call. Your staff represents your office in their responses, and you are responsible for appropriately training them to give correct responses.

PRESCRIBING CONTROLLED SUBSTANCES

Federal regulations[5] address prescribing controlled substances.[6] You must have a current DEA license to prescribe controlled substances, and some states require a state DEA license in addition. Check with your local medical society to determine any further regulations within your state. Controlled substances fall within

RUNNING YOUR OFFICE 75

five DEA categories, or "schedules."[7] Schedule I substances include drugs that have no accepted medical use in the United States and have a high potential for drug abuse, such as heroin, LSD, peyote, and mescaline. Schedule II substances have a high potential for drug abuse with a tendency toward severe psychic or physical dependence. Examples are certain narcotics, stimulants, and depressants, such as Demerol, Percodan, Ritalin, and barbiturates. Schedule III substances have a potential for drug abuse, but to a lesser degree than those in Schedules I and II. Examples are Doriden, Noludar, and Paregoric. Schedule IV substances have even less abuse potential than those listed in the previous schedules. Examples are Librium, Valium, and Darvon. Schedule V substances have minimal potential for drug abuse and consist primarily of compounds containing narcotic drugs for use as antitussives and antidiarrheals.

You must keep any controlled substances that you dispense from your office securely locked, and you must keep an accurate inventory, as well as detailed records of dispensation. To purchase drugs in Schedule II, you must obtain a purchase order from the DEA. Report any theft of controlled substances from your office to the DEA. For more information about regulation of controlled substances and about obtaining a DEA license, contact the United States Department of Justice, Drug Enforcement Administration, Registration Section, POB 28083, Central Station, Washington, D.C. 20005, (202) 633-1249 or visit the DEA Web site.[8]

PATIENT EDUCATION

Patients greatly appreciate time spent to help them understand their medical problems and treatment. Order relevant printed brochures from your specialty academy to give to your patients or print some of your own. Have available a VCR/TV in your office and educational tapes about different medical problems so that patients can learn more about their illnesses. A separate room for the VCR/TV is preferable so that a quiet atmosphere can be maintained in the waiting area for other patients. The VCR/TV can also be used to educate your staff on OSHA and CLIA regulations.

KEEPING UP

Remember that you must meet certain Continuing Medical Education (CME) requirements for license renewals. Check with your state medical society for these requirements and with your specialty association for a schedule of meetings that provide CME credits. Apart from these requirements, you will want of course to provide the best care possible to your patients. Remember to set aside some time each day for keeping up. Read an article from one of your specialty journals at home each evening, or while you are eating lunch. Journal clubs that are held monthly with others in your specialty are a good opportunity to discuss clinical problems and solutions and to forge good working relationships. Attend educational conferences each year. Keep textbooks handy in the office for reference, and always consult colleagues, within or outside of your specialty area as appropriate, on problems that stump you. Volunteer to lecture to groups, both medical and non-medical, as much as possible. You will learn as you teach. Keep up-to-date on new technologies relevant to running your office or treating your patients. Attend courses to learn new technologies, but also spend adequate time with other colleagues who use such technologies in their own offices, until you are comfortable with the technologies.

CONSULTATIONS AND REFERRALS

Be certain that your office staff transfers complete information to you regarding consults and referrals. Your staff should notify you when another physician calls, and you should see the consult or referral as quickly as possible and communicate in a timely manner to the referring or consulting physician.

DISABLED PATIENTS

Remember that your office should be accessible to patients with disabilities. The Americans with Disabilities Act (ADA) of 1990[9] prohibits against discrimination on the basis of disability and includes an obligation to make reasonable accommodations to meet the needs of patients or employees with disabilities.

COMMUNITY ACTIVITIES

Participate in your community. You can make a difference in promoting the health of your community through lectures, screening clinics, and training of other health care personnel. If there is a medical school in your community, offer to participate in resident training. Participate in hospital Grand Rounds where you have staff privileges and serve on hospital committees. You will be asked to talk to students about career plans, to lecture about medical problems, and to comment through the media on health issues. Your contribution to medicine can be far-reaching and very satisfying.

QUALITY OF PATIENT CARE

The quality of patient care is the most important aspect of running your office. Continuously update your knowledge and skills and always use the greatest diligence to make sure that you do everything possible to give your patients the care that they trust you to give. At the end of a long day it is very tempting to put off until later a chart dictation, a prescription refill or a request to return a phone call about a matter that does not appear urgent. Do everything that you know you should do before you leave the office at the end of the day. Small matters can suddenly turn into large problems. Take time to listen to your patients and to exercise all of your skills, both medical and managerial, to give your patients the highest quality of care.

Key Points

- The medical chart is a legal document.
- Always call in a chaperone when there is any doubt that a patient may be uncomfortable.
- It is best to have a chaperone if you are examining breast, genital, or anal areas.
- Collect co-payments due from the patient at the time of the visit.
- Consider wave scheduling.
- Return physician calls promptly.
- Send letters to referring or consulting physicians.
- Develop office policies.
- Train staff in emergency procedures.
- Maintain a current DEA license.
- Make your office accessible to patients with disabilities.
- Maintain the highest quality of patient care.

ENDNOTES

1. For electronic billing of Medicare see www.hcfa.gov/medicare/edi/edi.htm.
2. Available at www.hcfa.gov/medicare/edi/1500info.htm.
3. Available at www.hcfa.gov/medicare/edi/1500info.htm.
4. Available at www.ama-assn.org.
5. The Controlled Substances Act of 1970 (United States code Annotated Title 21, §811, et seq.).
6. For detailed information about these regulations, contact the Superintendent of Documents, U.S. Government Printing Office, Washington, D.C. 20402, (202) 783-3238.
7. See the DEA Web site available at www.usdoj.gov/dea/directory.htm for more information about Schedules I–V.
8. Available at www.usdoj.gov/dea.
9. Public Law 101-336, 42 U.S.C. §12101, et seq.

CHAPTER 11

Handling Difficult Patients

Your patients are your practice, and you will want to treat them with as much respect, kindness, efficiency, and expertise as possible. Most of them will think very highly of you and have full confidence in your treatment of their medical problems. By now you know, however, that there are some very difficult patients. You have had to deal with them in your residency, and you will have to deal with them in private practice. In private practice, the difference is that you won't rotate onto another service, leaving the problem patient to the next group of residents. The problem patient will be yours to keep, and you must continue to deal with the problems.

As you start up your practice you will inherit patients who are dissatisfied with their present doctors. Be very careful with them. You will not want to comment on their reasons for dissatisfaction with their doctors. You are hearing their side of the story, and you certainly do not want to magnify their perception of mistreatment or be quoted to the next doctor down the line as corroborating or giving sympathy to an exaggerated problem. Some of these patients will likely have outstanding debts in other physician offices. Do not despair. These patients will move on to other physician's offices, and your patient population will gradually become the group that you have hoped for.

Beware of the drug-seeking patient. This patient will often call you at night for a refill of a narcotic. Have the patient go to the emergency room for evaluation and ask the emergency room physician to call you regarding the evaluation. When you do write a prescription for a narcotic, be sure to write out in script, instead of only numerals, the number of pills that you are prescribing, as well as the number of refills. It is easy for a patient to add a digit or two to a prescription if you use numerals. Caution patients regarding side effects of medications, and indicate on the prescription appropriate warnings such as "may cause drowsiness; do not drive while taking." Also indicate briefly on the prescription the purpose of the medication (e.g., for blood pressure control) so that the patient will not confuse the medications.

In the meantime, continue to give your patients, difficult or not, good treatment, and document, document, document. It is vital in your everyday practice to carefully document what you have done for your patients and why. If you advise examination of certain areas, further testing or consultation and the patient declines, this should be documented. You should always discuss possible complications of a medication that you prescribe for a patient or a procedure that you are about to conduct, and you should document that you have discussed these possible complications with the patient. Your examination of the patient and your treatment plan should be carefully documented, and attempts to reschedule missed appointments should also be documented.

Above all, be available to your patients. Patient calls should be returned as soon as possible. Spend enough time with your patients to make sure that they feel that they have received good treatment and understand the treatment plan. Bad outcomes can happen even without negligence. Lawsuits can be filed even if there is no negligence. The plaintiff may not prevail, but much money, time, and heartache may be spent on the suit in the meantime. If your patients understand that you really care about them and that you are doing your best for them, they will be less likely to consider filing lawsuits.

Even with the best of schedules, you will encounter the patient that comes in with not one but five problems that the patient feels are critical. Sometimes there are underlying issues related to personal problems or stress, and the patient feels the need to talk about these problems. You'll listen sympathetically to the patient's concerns. You will treat the medical problems, answer the patient's questions, explain the patient's medical problems and your medical treatment, distinguish the medical from the non-medical problems, and do your best to alleviate concerns. You will recommend counseling as necessary. But you will have fallen far behind in your schedule, and the waiting patients may be disgruntled.

Some patients will have left. Others later may write you letters of complaint. A few may change physicians. What could you have done differently? Balance your time with your patients as best as possible. Address the medical problems necessary to treat at the time. Refer the patient as necessary to those best able to help with the patient's problems outside of your area of expertise. Keep handy a list of physicians to whom you refer patients with office phone numbers and addresses. Refer the patient for counseling if the patient has stressful emotional problems. Schedule a follow-up visit to further discuss non-critical problems within your specialty area that you cannot address within the time scheduled. Explain to your patient that you would like to further discuss issues of concern to the patient to determine a plan of action and would like to have more time to do so. If you are still running late, relax. You have done your best. You cannot always see everyone exactly on time.

Patients who write letters to you complaining about your staff or your lack of promptness should receive a response from you that is brief but polite, thanking them for letting you know about their inconvenience, apologizing to them, if warranted, for their inconvenience, and expressing hope that they will not have an unpleasant experience again. Correct any problems as necessary. If the letter is unwarranted, respond politely but appropriately. For example, if they were accommodated as a walk-in patient and had to wait, explain briefly that persons with unscheduled appointments may have to wait. Your staff should be careful to explain this when unscheduled patients call and are put into the schedule as walk-ins.

Occasionally you and your office staff will encounter "patient rage." Sometimes the staff will receive the brunt of the rage and you will enter the exam room to find a calm patient. At other times the rage will continue. Patient rage may be precipitated by a specific situational event, such as having to wait too long to see the doctor, and/or it may be a manifestation of an underlying psychosis or borderline psychological disorder. It is very important that you have an office policy discussing patient rage, its dangers, and steps to be taken when one of your employees encounters patient rage. You should discuss this policy with your staff and make certain that all understand what to do when they encounter this problem.

Think carefully about the steps that you would like your employees to take and obtain their feedback and suggestions. If the patient hostility appears to stem from a particular situation, such as having to wait too long for the doctor, the staff member should listen in an interested, polite manner to the complaint, acknowledge the frustration of the patient, and offer a solution, such as rescheduling. If it is unclear if a particular situation has stimulated the rage, if the situation does not appear improved by offering a solution, or if the employee has any doubts as to his or her safety, the employee should notify you immediately. You should listen calmly to the patient and assess the situation, reassure the patient about your interest in his or her welfare, and offer a solution if possible. Never underestimate potential danger to you or your staff from patient rage, and call security if necessary.

Finally, you will on occasion encounter an extremely difficult patient that you can help in a way that is very important to him or her, and the patient will transform into your most loyal and trusting patient. You will see the patient's life change as a result of your help, and you will feel that this is more of a reward for going into medicine than you could have imagined. This is the patient that you will remember most and hold in your heart.

Key Points
- Caution patients about side effects of medications.
- Be available to your patients.
- Have an office policy for addressing patient rage.
- Never underestimate the potential danger to you or your staff from a hostile patient.

CHAPTER **12**

Health Care Compliance with Federal Regulations

It is very important to understand federal regulations that impact the practice of medicine. The federal government has made substantial efforts in the past few years to detect what it considers fraud and abuse. The government has focused especially on Medicare claims to determine whether the service billed for a patient visit was medically necessary and supported by documentation, but the federal government can prosecute for improper claims involving any health care benefit program.[1]

Many different things can trigger a federal audit of your charts. A common trigger is a senior citizen who believes that you have charged Medicare or Medicaid for a service that has not been rendered. "Senior Patrols," sponsored by the Administration on Aging act as the eyes and ears of the Medicare beneficiary system for the federal government. Be sure to explain carefully to your patients the procedures that you are doing and why.

What do federal agents look for in their audits? Fraud[2] is defined by the Health Care Financing Administration (HCFA)[3] as "knowingly and willfully executing, or attempting to execute, a scheme or artifice to defraud any health care benefit program or to obtain, by means of false or fraudulent pretenses, representations, or promises, any of the money or property owned by, or under the custody or control of, any health care benefit program." Examples of fraud are billing for services not rendered, using an incorrect provider number in billing, signing blank records used by another entity to obtain Medicare payment, offering incentives to Medicare patients not offered to non-Medicare patients, such as waiving the Medicare deductible or co-pay, falsifying any information on medical records or billing statements, or misrepresenting as medically necessary non-covered screening services by using inappropriate procedure or diagnosis codes.

Abuse[4] is defined by HCFA as actions that may, "directly or indirectly, result in unnecessary costs to the Medicare or Medicaid program, improper payment, or payment for services which fail to meet professionally recognized standards of care, or that are medically unnecessary." Abuse involves payment for services when there is no legal entitlement to that payment and when the provider has knowingly misrepresented facts to obtain such payment. Examples of abuse are using procedure codes that describe services more extensive than those actually performed, collecting more than the twenty percent co-payment or deductible on claims filed to Medicare, requiring a deposit from a Medicare beneficiary as a condition for care, billing for clinical laboratory tests that were performed by another entity, billing for services grossly in excess of those needed by patients, and threatening to evict a Medicare beneficiary receiving in-patient services due to an inability to pay a Medicare deductible or co-insurance.

You must not bill Medicare or Medicaid for medically unnecessary services. Medicare does not cover services that are not reasonable and necessary for diagnosis and treatment of an illness or injury. Among non-covered services are routine physicals and cosmetic services. Be sure to inform your patients if a service is medically unnecessary and therefore will not be covered by Medicare.[5] If a Medicare patient wants you to treat a problem that is cosmetic, you will need to have the patient sign a waiver stating that he or she understands that the problem is cosmetic and not covered by Medicare, that Medicare will therefore not be billed, and that the patient will be responsible for payment for the cosmetic treatment.

Federal agents and auditors will also look for unbundling. Unbundling is separate billing of procedures that should be billed together as a single charge. Separating the procedures into the separate charges results in greater cost to the Medicare program. Medicare regulations specify which procedures are relevant to this regulation.

It is evident that a medical biller of good quality or a good billing service is important to a medical office. But it is still important to learn how to code correctly and to periodically check that the biller is doing his or her job correctly. HCFA holds providers responsible for their claims even when they use billing services or consultants. So do learn how to code the services that you render and periodically check that coding is done correctly. Saying that you didn't know about these regulations won't work with the federal government. HCFA has made it known that ignorance about changes in Medicare billing requirements is not a defense. Providers are not only responsible for the quality of the health care that they or their organizations render, but they are also responsible for knowing current Medicare billing requirements and billing correctly. Cross-train your office staff so that they can check one another on correct coding. You must promptly reimburse Medicare for any amount over-billed. On the positive side, you may discover that your biller is under-coding or that compensation is delayed due to incorrect billing. Corrections of these problems can result in significant income improvement.

Be careful to date your patient encounter notes; if you bill for services rendered for a date not documented in the chart and the government audits your charts, the government will consider a bill for these services fraudulent. Be careful not to certify any medical equipment as necessary for a patient unless it is truly medically necessary and not just a convenience.

Be sure the elements documented in the chart are sufficient for the level of service coded and billed. This is important. Evaluation and management guidelines have been developed by HCFA to indicate the necessary elements to document. You should become familiar with the guidelines listed on the AMA[6] or HCFA[7] Web sites and monitor for changes. Learn to bill correctly while in your residency. Attend a coding course offered by your specialty association prior to going into practice. Send your office staff periodically to coding/billing courses so that they will be up-to-date on changes. Fines and penalties for medical fraud or abuse are staggering, and imprisonment is possible.[8] You should not underestimate the importance of learning to bill correctly, whether in your own practice or working as an employee in a practice.

Health care facilities must comply with anti-reassignment regulations, anti-kickback regulations, Stark II, COBRA, CLIA, OSHA, and DEA regulations, anti-discrimination laws, and other federal and state laws. Anti-reassignment regulations prohibit assigning a physician's right to receive Medicare pay to a billing agent if the billing agent receives a percentage of the amount collected. The anti-kickback statute prohibits the "knowing payment of anything of value to influence referral of federal health care program business, including Medicare and Medicaid,"[9] such as incentive pay by a hospital to a physician when the physician refers a patient to the hospital. The Consolidated Omnibus Budget Reconciliation Act (COBRA)[10] requires employers with twenty or more employees to extend group health plan coverage to terminated employees and their beneficiaries for up to 36 months. The Omnibus Budget Reconciliation Act of 1993 (Stark II)[11] prohibits physicians from making referrals to entities with which they have a financial relationship. Health care facilities must also comply with CLIA, OSHA, and DEA regulations and anti-discrimination laws, which are discussed elsewhere in this book.

Medicare considers offering incentives to Medicare patients that are not offered to non-Medicare patients an example of Medicare fraud. Examples include routinely waiving or discounting the Medicare deductible or co-insurance amounts. If you advertise certain free services to attract patients to your office, you cannot then bill such services to Medicare or secondary insurers of the patient. Nor can you routinely waive patients' Medicare co-payments and tell the patients that you'll just bill Medicare, or Medicare and a secondary insurance. These practices are unlawful. You can, however, waive co-insurance or deductibles in unusual instances of extreme financial hardship. You must document such information in the patient record.

Be careful about professional courtesy. This can be considered violation of the anti-kickback law. The AMA Policy on professional courtesy states, "Physicians should exercise caution in extending professional courtesy where the patient may be in a position to make referrals. If the physician's intent behind extending professional courtesy is to generate referrals for Medicare or Medicaid covered services, the government will be in a position to prosecute a fraud or abuse case for a violation of the anti-kickback law."[12]

The federal government expects medical offices to develop a compliance plan that illustrates steps taken by the office to insure compliance with Federal Regulations. You can find many Web sites that offer to develop a compliance plan for your office, but

88 GOING INTO MEDICAL PRACTICE

you can easily develop your own. The Office of Inspector General (OIG) has issued guidelines for hospitals for a compliance plan. These guidelines can be found on the OIG Web site at www.usda.gov/oig/ and can be adapted and modified as appropriate into a compliance plan for a medical office. Another helpful Web site for information on compliance issues is the HCFA Web site at www.hcfa.gov.

Your office compliance plan should reflect a working compliance program of your practice. The plan must be in writing and must be well known and used by every member of the practice. The plan need not be complex and can be modified as new and better ways of effecting compliance are developed by the practice. It should include a mission statement that reflects the commitment of the practice to ensure that its affairs are conducted in accordance with applicable law. Delineate goals for accomplishing the mission, such as ensuring that claims to the government and private payers are true and accurate; listing your office procedures for identifying, investigating, disciplining, and preventing unethical conduct; and describing your programs for regular training and education of physicians and other staff. The plan should reflect the following compliance efforts: Education should be regular and appropriate to ensure correct documentation, billing, and collection as well as to ensure compliance with other regulated activities.[13] A method that encourages employees to report potential problems should be developed, and procedures should be included that direct prompt investigation and handling of compliance problems. Audits should be conducted periodically to determine if the compliance program is effective. Written standards of conduct, policies, and procedures to promote the organization's commitment to compliance should be developed as part of the plan and distributed to all members of the practice. Periodic quality assurance (QA) meetings should be held to update the policies contained within the plan, to review the overall compliance effort, and to discuss any issues that have arisen.

Such actions will not only promote federally mandated compliance, but will create more office efficiency, result in more control over office billing and collections functions, and provide more protection from legal and federal problems by enhanced documentation.[14]

CLIA

In 1988, Congress passed the Clinical Laboratory Improvement Amendments (CLIA),[15] which establish standards of quality for all laboratory testing on human specimens. Laboratory testing includes examination of specimens by microscope and performing hemocult tests or dipstick urine tests. A physician office or any other facility that performs such testing is considered a laboratory for purposes of CLIA. The Health Care Financing Agency (HCFA) is responsible for oversight of CLIA implementation, including overseeing registration of laboratories, collecting fees, conducting surveys, developing guidelines, and enforcing CLIA regulations.

The type of CLIA license that you need depends upon the complexity of the tests that you run in your laboratory. There are three categories of tests:

1. low complexity
2. moderate complexity, including the subcategory of provider-performed microscopy (PPM), and
3. high complexity.

You must register with the Department of Health and Human Services (DHHS) and obtain a certificate and CLIA number. It is important to know that all laboratories must register with DHHS and obtain a CLIA certificate regardless of whether or not the laboratory receives payment from Medicare, Medicaid, or any other third party payer.

Procedures such as examination of wet mounts, including vaginal, cervical, or skin specimens and examination of all potassium hydroxide (KOH) preparations, fall within the category of provider-performed microscopy (PPM) procedures. To be categorized as a PPM procedure, a physician must personally perform the examination on a specimen obtained from the patient, or a qualified midlevel practitioner must perform the exam under the supervision of a physician. Laboratories that perform only low complexity tests or PPM tests as part of a patient exam are exempt from routine inspection by HCFA. To obtain a list of procedures categorized as low, moderate (including PPM tests), or high complexity, access the Web site ftp.cdc.gov/pub/laboratory_info/clia.

To enroll in the CLIA program, a laboratory must complete an application, pay a fee depending upon the category of tests performed, and be inspected by HCFA if applicable to the category (inspection not necessary for low complexity and PPM categories). One of the following certificates would then be issued as appropriate:

1. Certificate of Waiver;
2. Certificate for provider-performed microscopy (PPM) procedures;
3. Certificate of Registration (issued to a laboratory; it enables the laboratory to conduct moderate or high complexity laboratory testing until the laboratory is determined by survey to be in compliance with the CLIA);
4. Certificate of Compliance (issued to a laboratory after an inspection finds the laboratory in compliance with CLIA regulations);
5. Certificate of Accreditation (issued to a laboratory on the basis of the laboratory's accreditation by an accreditation organization approved by HCFA).

After receiving a certificate, a laboratory performing moderate or high complexity tests is usually inspected by HCFA every two years. Contact HCFA at www.hcfa.gov for an application and for more information.

OSHA

In 1970, Congress established the Occupational Safety and Health Administration (OSHA) to assure safe working conditions. OSHA has developed standards and requirements for the workplace that it enforces through inspections.

OSHA requires employers to develop effective safety programs for the workplace and to educate office personnel in these programs. Physicians must put into place and maintain systems for adequate cleaning of surfaces to prevent contamination, effective decontamination of instruments and equipment, protection of eyes, protection of food, safe operation of lasers, quality control of autoclaves and other instruments, and correct disposal of needles and other contaminated materials. To learn about infectious waste management regulations, contact your local hospital to determine the agency in your state that deals with medical waste.

An office must develop its own plan for compliance with OSHA standards. An OSHA kit that is helpful in setting up an OSHA compliance plan can be obtained from most medical supply companies. Medical supply companies can also provide you with information on obtaining OSHA-required labels and signs. When in doubt about what or where to buy these or any other medical products, check with your local hospital's purchasing department.

You should include a Bloodborne Pathogen Exposure Control Plan in your OSHA compliance plan. Include a list of your office employees, their job classification, and whether in performance of their duties they could reasonably be at risk for skin, eye, mucous membrane, or parenteral contact with blood or other potentially infectious material. Those at risk should be offered, at no charge to themselves, vaccination for hepatitis B. You can obtain information on current recommendations related to prevention of hepatitis B from the Centers for Disease Control, Hepatitis Branch, 1600 Clifton Road, NE, Atlanta, GA 30333, (404) 639-2709. Discuss with staff at risk the risks and seriousness of hepatitis B, and if they decline vaccination knowing such risks, have them sign a statement indicating that they have been offered the vaccination and decline the offer, understanding the risks of hepatitis B. Keep such statements in your OSHA file. You can obtain copies of CDC recommendations on universal precautions and prevention of HIV transmission in health care settings from the CDC Hospital Infections Web site at **aepo-xdv-www.epo.cdc.gov**.[16]

Describe in your plan the areas where exposure to bloodborne pathogens might occur and describe the cleaning and decontamination schedules for all such areas. Describe in detail the procedures to follow if such exposure occurs. The procedures should include washing exposed skin surfaces with water, flushing exposed mucous membranes, reporting the incident, and following up appropriately. Also include in your OSHA compliance plan a record of staff attendance at an OSHA training program that you have conducted in order for each employee to discuss danger of, and protection from, bloodborne pathogens. The AMA has developed a training kit, "For Your Protection: The OSHA Regulations on Bloodborne Pathogens," that can be obtained by calling (800) 933-4AMT or through the AMA Web site at www.ama-assn.org. Your staff should be well trained in the use of any emergency equipment in the office. Include this information in your office policy manual for assisting in training of new employees and for reference. Such equipment should be periodically checked to make sure that it is operational. Include in your OSHA compliance plan your staff-training plan for use of such equipment.

For more information about OSHA and its mandates, see the OSHA Web site at www.osha.gov. Be sure to review this Web site carefully. You can also obtain information from the OSHA Office of Publications, U.S. Department of Labor, Room N3101, 200 Constitution Avenue, N.W., Washington, D.C. 20210, (202) 523-9667.

FEDERAL TRADE COMMISSION

The Federal Trade Commission (FTC) is involved in two areas of particular relevance to the practice of medicine. The first area involves truth in advertising. The FTC wants to protect the consumer from misleading advertising. Any advertising by the medical profession must be truthful and capable of substantiation. Claims regarding cosmetic procedures are particularly scrutinized to make certain that a truthful picture is presented about possible complications and potential discomfort, as well as expected outcomes. If you advertise, make sure that your claims of benefits do not go beyond the truth and that you can substantiate these claims.

The second area of concern of the FTC is restraint of trade. The FTC encourages healthy competition among health care providers so that the public can benefit from competitive prices for health care. The FTC is on the lookout for price fixing, where a group of specialists agree to charge certain prices for certain procedures. The FTC also watches for consolidations of practices, hospitals, or other arrangements among health care organizations that could reduce competition in an area. Organizations thinking about merging can obtain an advisory opinion from the FTC, which will consider potential benefits and detriments to the public from such a merger. As your practice grows, you may consider merging with other offices. Involve your attorney to make certain that not only do you benefit by the arrangement but also that the arrangement does not violate FTC regulations regarding restraint of trade. The FTC Web site is located at **www.ftc.gov**.

Key Points

- Understand federal regulations that impact the practice of medicine.
- A common trigger for a federal audit is a senior citizen who believes that Medicare or Medicaid has been billed for a service not rendered.
- Fraud as defined by HCFA includes billing for services not rendered and billing for medically unnecessary services or routinely waiving or discounting the Medicare deductible or co-payment.
- Abuse as defined by HCFA includes upcoding and billing for services in excess of those needed by patients.
- Date your patient encounter notes.
- The elements of care documented in the chart must be sufficient for the level of service coded and billed.
- Learn to bill correctly while in your residency.
- Develop an office plan for compliance with federal regulations.
- You must register with HHS and obtain a CLIA certificate.
- OSHA has developed standards and requirements for the workplace that OSHA enforces through inspections.
- The FTC monitors truth in advertising and prohibits restraint of trade.

ENDNOTES

1. The Health Insurance Portability and Accountability Act of 1996 (Kassebaum-Kennedy Act) 18 USC §1347 (1997) defines federal health care fraud to include "any health care benefit program."
2. Lewis CL. Fraud and Abuse: Protect Yourself. Blue Cross Blue Shield of Florida, Inc. Government Programs Division. Medicare Fraud & Abuse. Document Number CPT1.1. (1998); 86.
3. Available at www.hcfa.gov.
4. Lewis CL. Fraud and Abuse: Protect Yourself. Blue Cross Blue Shield of Florida, Inc. Government Programs Division. Medicare Fraud & Abuse. Document Number CPT1.1. (1998); 86.
5. See the HCFA Web site, available at www.hcfa.gov/medicare/fraud, for more information about fraud and abuse.
6. Available at www.ama-assn.org.
7. Available at www.hcfa.gov/audience/planprov.htm.
8. See www.ama-assn.org/physlegl/legal/doc1d.htm for some of the penalties for fraud and abuse.
9. Available at www.dhhs.gov/progorg/oig/ak/safenr.htm.
10. 66 Federal Register 7 (2001).

11. 1993 amendments to the Stark Law; pub Fed. Register Jan. 8, 1998.
12. Available at www.ama-assn.org/physlegl/legal/patphys.htm.
13. AMA News, Oct. 12, 1998; Howard Kim.
14. For additional information relevant to compliance, see www.floridamedicare.com, a computer-based training module on fraud and abuse, and the HHS Web site at www.hhs.gov. Other Web sites include Corporate Compliance Home Page at www.corporatecompliance.com; Compliance Programs and the Corporate Sentencing Guidelines at www.carswell.com/records/CPG.html; Office of Inspector General at www.sbanonline.sba.gov/ignet/internal/hhs/hhs.html; Health Care Financing Administration at www.hcfa.gov; Qui tam case information by Taxpayers Against Fraud at www.taf.org; and the Federal Register's Web site at www.access.gpo.gov/su_docs/aces/aces140.html. For information about membership in the Health Care Compliance Association, call (888) 580-8373.
15. www.hcfa.gov/medicaid/clia/cliahome.htm.
16. Also see the CDC Web site at www.phppo.cdc.gov.

CHAPTER **13**

Legal and Ethical Considerations: Avoiding Liability

Once you begin treatment of a patient at the patient's request, a doctor-patient relationship arises with certain legal obligations. There are also ethical considerations that, while not codified in law, are important to your patient, to risk management and to the practice of medicine in general.

When a doctor-patient relationship arises, you have a legal obligation to provide medically appropriate care. You may not terminate care of the patient without reasonable notice to the patient, so that the patient will have an opportunity to obtain alternative care. What if a patient continues to refuse to pay his or her bill? Notify the patient in writing, by certified letter, that you are terminating care. Give the reason and the date that termination of your care to the patient will occur. Make sure that you have given the patient adequate time to find alternative care, and indicate in the letter that, at the patient's written request, you will send the patient's records to the physician that the patient may designate. Keep the return receipt from the certified letter on file.

Remember that you must always have the patient's signed consent before transferring the patient's medical record to another physician. This is an important legal issue of confidentiality. You must not reveal confidences entrusted to you by the patient.

You have a legal duty to adequately inform your patient about any medical treatment that you plan to give to the patient. You must give the reason for treatment, the risks, alternatives to treatment, and possible consequences of no treatment. Make sure that the patient has an opportunity to ask any questions and that the patient consents to the treatment. Ask the patient to sign a consent form before initiating a procedure. Make certain that you have discussed the form with the patient and that the patient understands the procedure. If the patient is incompetent, you must have the consent of the next of kin or of a guardian. If a patient is a minor, you must have the consent of a parent. If the parents of a minor are divorced, you must have the consent of the parent who has custody. In life-saving emergencies, parents cannot usually refuse treatment of a child if treatment would be beneficial and if the prognosis with treatment is good. State laws may differ in some matters regarding consent.

You must keep your medical records, even if you decide to close your office. If you close your office, send a letter to each of your patients notifying of the closing and offering to send the patient's records to the physician that the patient may designate by written request. Not only may your patients need access to their medical records, but federal authorities may still audit your records, and should any lawsuits be filed against you, you must have the relevant medical records. Although your state's statute of limitations may limit the time in which a suit may be filed, in certain cases the statute may be suspended, expanding significantly the period of time for filing a suit. This may occur, for example, when a minor is involved or when fraud is alleged. State laws differ; clarify your specific legal obligations with your attorney. Contact your state medical society for legislation affecting the practice of medicine within your state.

The American Medical Association (AMA) is an excellent resource for all physicians. The AMA Web site[1] lists current opinions on legal and ethical issues[2] and includes standards addressing confidentiality, informed consent, ending the physician-patient relationship, professional courtesy, waiver of co-pay, and responsibilities to the hearing-disabled patient. The AMA Web site also contains references to health care attorneys and to consultants for developing an office. The AMA is actively involved in developing coding guidelines. You can send your input to the AMA through your specialty academy, which works with the AMA on these and other HCFA interactions. If you disagree with federal laws, contact the AMA litigation section to express your ideas for constructive changes.

MEDICAL MALPRACTICE

No one wants to be sued, but anyone can file a suit. The plaintiff may not prevail, but he or she can cost you precious time and money and cause headache and heartache. You can lessen the chances that you will be sued by having a good relationship with your patients, and you can lessen the chances that you will be sued successfully by being aware of the duties that arise because of the physician-patient relationship.

In order for a patient (plaintiff) to prevail in a lawsuit against you that claims negligence, the patient must show that you had a duty to him or her to render non-negligent care, that you breached that duty, and that this breach caused harm to the patient. All of these elements must be present for the patient to prevail. Actions have also been brought against physicians for breach of contract. Never guarantee to a patient that a particular result will occur from a treatment.

Let's suppose that a lawsuit claiming negligence is filed by one of your patients, naming you as the defendant. First ask, did you have a duty to the patient? Yes. Once you begin treatment of a patient at the patient's request, a doctor-patient relationship arises with the duty to render non-negligent care. Second, did you render non-negligent or negligent care? If you were not negligent, you rendered that level of care that a member in good standing in your specialty would provide under similar circumstances. Expert witnesses, who are usually members of your specialty, would be called in court to testify as to that level of care. Finally, if your care was negligent, did harm result, and was the negligent care the proximal cause of the harm? Would the harm not have occurred but for your actions? Was the harm reasonably foreseeable by you? Did you take reasonable steps to protect the patient from the harm? These are the questions that a court would consider.

Consult your attorney when there is any doubt about how to handle a matter legally. If a lawsuit is filed that names you as a defendant, contact your attorney immediately. You should never go back and alter a medical record, even if you feel that you need to clarify something in the record. Plaintiff's attorneys could use a changed record to destroy your credibility in court. What happens if, in the course of your practice, you notice a typographical error in a medical record that may be misleading? You can cross out the error so that you can still see what was originally written, write in the correction, then initial and date the change. Never use white-out or mark through the error to the extent that you cannot see what was originally written. Do nothing to a record that relates to a lawsuit that has been filed.

Develop a good relationship with your patients. Most lawsuits are filed by patients who are dissatisfied with a patient-physician relationship. Respond promptly to calls by your patients, make certain that your patients can always reach you or the covering physician, and involve your patients in informed decisions about their care.

> ### Key Points
> - In order for a patient (plaintiff) to prevail in a lawsuit against you that claims negligence, the patient must show that you had a duty to him or her to render non-negligent care, that you breached that duty, and that this breach caused harm to the patient. All of these elements must be present for the patient to prevail.
> - Never terminate care of a patient without reasonable notice.
> - Obtain a patient's signed consent before transferring the patient's medical record to another physician.
> - Inform the patient of treatment and procedures and obtain his or her consent.
> - Always consult an attorney when there is any doubt about how to legally handle a matter.

ENDNOTES

1. Available at www.ama-assn.org/physlegl/legal/patphys.htm.
2. See the AMA's Code of Medical Ethics available at www.ama-assn.org/physlegl/legal/patphys.htm.

CHAPTER 14

Insurance

As discussed earlier in this book, you will need malpractice (professional liability) insurance as of the day that you begin practicing medicine. As discussed in Chapter 3, there are generally two types of malpractice insurance: occurrence-based and claims-made. Occurrence insurance provides coverage for malpractice claims filed at any time for acts occurring during the coverage period. Claims-made insurance provides coverage only for claims filed during the coverage period. Occurrence insurance is more expensive than claims-made insurance. If you discontinue claims-made coverage, however, you will need to purchase expensive "tail" insurance to protect against any claims filed after the coverage period for acts that occurred during the coverage period. The cost of malpractice insurance differs with different medical specialties and in different states. Check with your professional organizations about obtaining group rates.

You are likely to already have auto, health, life, and home insurance. If you set up your own office, however, you will need other insurance specific to your office and practice.

You will, for example, need insurance for office liability and office contents. You may also need to contribute to workers compensation insurance. Check with your state medical society or state worker's compensation board to determine whether your state requires this.[1] What if you find down the road that one of your trusted employees has been taking money from the practice? You may want to consider, at the beginning of your practice, a fidelity bond that will insure against losses due to a dishonest employee. What about unforeseen catastrophes to your office building and your patient records? There is insurance that will compensate for loss of profits if your office building is damaged and for inability to collect accounts receivables in case the medical records are destroyed.

You will need disability insurance in case you should suddenly become disabled. Disability insurance will replace income lost because of your disability. Investigate different policies before you settle upon one. Check to see how much income will be replaced, after what waiting period, and under what conditions. Check with your local medical society and your professional organizations to see what disability policies are offered to members at group rates. Look to see up to what age and under what conditions the policy is renewable, whether occupation protection under the plan refers to your ability to practice your own specialty and not your ability to practice medicine in general, whether premiums are waived if you become totally disabled, what benefits are included for nondisabling injuries such as fractures, dislocations, and accidental loss of limbs, and whether rehabilitation provisions are included.

If you have your own office, you will also need office overhead insurance. Should you become disabled, your major medical insurance will help pay your medical bills and your liability insurance will provide income, but you will need office overhead insurance to cover the cost of maintaining your office while you are disabled. Office overhead insurance will pay utility bills and other fixed business expenses, including payment of salaries to your employees as they continue to staff the office, bill for services rendered, and collect accounts receivables.

There is a wide range of insurance plans and options. What do you really need? You should contact an insurance agent who has been recommended by another medical office and discuss the advantages and costs of the different types of insurance. Before deciding, contact your accountant for advice about what types of insurance you should have and how much you will need.

The AMA Web site[2] includes information on evaluating a professional liability insurance policy,[3] as well as liability insurance requirements for different states.

> **Key Points**
>
> - You will need malpractice insurance as of the day that you begin practicing medicine.
> - There are generally two types of malpractice insurance: occurrence and claims-made.
> - If you have your own office, you will need insurance for office liability and office contents as well as office overhead insurance.
> - You will need disability insurance.

ENDNOTES

1. See the Small Business Association Web site at **www.sba.gov/starting** for states that require contribution to workers compensation insurance.
2. Available at **www.ama-assn.org/physlegl/legal/profins.htm**.
3. Also see the AMA publication, *Medical Professional Liability Insurance*, available through the AMA Physician Catalog (at **www.ama-assn.org/physlegl/legal/profins.htm**).

CHAPTER **15**

Academic Medicine

The focus thus far has been on going into private practice. Before settling upon the best situation for you, however, it is important to consider the practice of medicine within an academic setting. The need for optimum interactions with your patients remains the same as in private practice, as well as the need to code correctly, to comply with federal regulations, to handle difficult patients successfully, to avoid legal difficulties, and to uphold ethical standards. Although each academic situation is unique, there are some general differences between the private and the academic practice setting.

If you affiliate with an academic medical center, you likely will be closer to the cutting edge of new technologies and therapies. You will be able to participate in grand rounds and special programs within the academic institution that probably would be more difficult to attend while in private practice. You will have the benefit of daily interactions with colleagues. You will not feel distant from the mainstream as one can feel in private practice. You also can interact easily with colleagues in other specialties and attend seminars in other fields to keep up with areas outside of your specialty. You likely will be able to refer your patients more efficiently to these colleagues for care as necessary.

You probably will make less money than in private practice, but malpractice insurance may be paid for by the academic institute, and you may have other benefits such as group health insurance policies, retirement plans, paid vacation, and subsidy for travel to meetings. You likely will share your knowledge at meetings and in publications, and you may find that you are involved in efforts within your academic institution and the national medical community to develop policies, regulations, and goals.

You will have the satisfaction of being able to make a difference in health care in general as well as in the health of your patients. Of course you can influence health care while you are in private practice, but schedules in academic medicine are more likely to allow time for such efforts.

You will find, however, that administrative responsibilities result in less time to spend with your patients. You may see patients only a few days during the week and spend the other days carrying out administrative responsibilities. Your days may be longer. The usual day may not end when the last patient leaves and the daily follow-up of patient care is completed. You may have policies to draft, a late meeting to attend, a speech to prepare, and a publication to send to the publishers.

There can be great satisfaction in practicing within an academic medical center. It is a perfect setting for some physicians but not for others. If you are interested in academic medicine, talk with your colleagues who practice within this setting to determine whether it is right for you.

Key Points

- If you affiliate with an academic medical center, you will be closer to the cutting edge of new technologies and therapies.
- You probably will make less money than in private practice.
- You will have benefits such as participation in group health insurance plans and retirement plans.

CHAPTER **16**

Enjoying Your Practice

Whether you have your own practice or join a group, you are about to make your dream of practicing medicine come true. It is true that the practice of medicine is not the same as it once was, and this is positive as well as negative. Managed care may complicate medical practice, but at the same time there are new technologies and treatments, both available now and on the horizon, that can dramatically improve the course of medical treatment. Keep up with the new changes and new technologies. Make them available to your patients through your own practice or through referral to appropriate sources. You will have the kind of power to treat and heal your patients that could not have been imagined in the past.

Some things, however, have not changed over time. Giving your patients the highest quality of care, having compassion for your patients, perceiving problems beyond those that are apparent, and giving your patients a better self-image through your care can make a significant difference in their lives, and in your life. The moments when you made a difference in someone's life are the ones that you will remember down the road.

The treatment that you give may seem insignificant to you, but may in fact have a huge impact. Years ago I was seeing students in a clinic at a small southern college. I walked into an exam room to find an angry student accompanied by a policeman. The boy had been caught selling drugs and was awaiting trial. The policeman was waiting to escort him back to the school stockade. The boy had a deep scowl across his face, and his belligerent words to me were, "You can't do anything to help me!"

I knew that he was right. I could treat the angry red and purple acne cysts that had erupted over his cheeks and even the venereal warts that he had, but I couldn't do anything about his drug arrest or his other problems. I couldn't put his life back together for him. Treating acne and warts must have seemed like an insult in view of the huge problems that he faced.

"You may be right," I said. "But I can try to help your acne if you want me to."

His anger at the world was reflected in his tense stance, in his face half averted from me, and in his deep scowl. Like a sullen child he did not answer. Finally he shrugged his shoulders in frustrated resignation. For one fleeting moment I saw a flicker of what could have been hope in his eyes, but it was quickly extinguished and replaced again by defiance.

I saw him in the clinic four times over the next eight weeks. His defiance gradually lessened as his acne and warts began to clear up with treatment.

His fourth visit was my last time in the clinic. I was rotating to another clinic the following week. The boy was quiet. His complexion was blemish free, and he was quite handsome. His warts were gone. I had to feel satisfied with the results of the medical treatment even if I could not help him with his larger problems.

"Goodbye, and good luck," I said.

As I turned to leave the exam room, I heard him say softly, "Doctor?" I turned back toward him.

"Thank you," he said quietly.

That moment has stayed with me forever. You have all had or will have a moment when a patient's gratitude lets you know that your treatment has been more significant to the patient than you could have imagined. And all of your training becomes worthwhile in that one moment.

Good Luck!

Key Points

- Keep up with new changes and new technologies and make them available to your patients.
- The treatment that you give may seem insignificant to you, but may have more of an impact than you can imagine.

APPENDIX A

Suggested Reading: Books on Practice Management

Bujold EJ. The Fifteen Minute Office Practice Manager: How to Run a Successful Medical Office Practice, Speck Publishing (1999), 30 p.
Buck CJ, Lovaasen KR, Green MA. Step-By-Step Medical Coding, W.B. Saunders (2000), 622 p.
Fox YM, Levine BA. How to Join, Buy, or Merge a Physician's Practice (1998), 397 p.
Fox YM. How to Manage the Business Called Private Practice, What They Didn't Teach You in Medical School. Janice Nagano, Ed. (1994), 380 p.
Hamburg J (Ed.). Merriam-Webster's Medical Office Handbook. Merriam-Webster (1996), 544 p.
Kramer DC. Medical Practice Management. (Boston, MA) Little, Brown and Company (1982).
McCue JD. Private Practice: Surviving the First Year. (Lexington, MA) The Collamore Press (1982).
Reiholdt, Max. American Medical Association (AMA). Starting a Medical Practice. The Physician's Handbook for Successful Practice Start-up. (Norcross, Georgia) Coker Publishing Company, LLC (1996).
Silver JK. The Successful Physician, Aspen Publishers, 1st Ed. (1998), 107 p.
Silver JK. The Business of Medicine. Hanley and Belfus (1998).
Tinsley R. Medical Practice Management Handbook 2000: Policy Guide to Accounting and Tax Issues, Daily Operations, and Physicians' Contracts. Harcourt Brace (2000), 900 p.
Tinsley R, Havens JD. Performing an Operational and Strategic Assessment for a Medical Practice. John Wiley & Sons (1999).
Winer RR. Practice Management for the Physician. (Akron, Ohio) Winer & Bevilacqua, Inc, 2nd Ed. (1996).
Zaslove MO. The Successful Physician: A Productivity Handbook for Practitioners (1998), 307 p.

APPENDIX B

Helpful Web Sites

ACLS, BLS, PALS

BLS/CPR: www.cpr-ecc.org
ACLS: www.acls.net
ACLS, BLS, PALS: www.proeducation.com/ecc/T_courses/Tcor_ACLS.htm

AMA

AMA Web site: www.ama-assn.org

BILLING

Medicare Electronic Billing: www.hcfa.gov/medicare/edi/edi.htm
HCFA 1500 forms for submitting paper billing:
www.hcfa.gov/medicare/edi/1500info.htm

BUSINESS

Information on starting and operating a small business:
IRS Web site at www.irs.ustreas.gov/bus_info
Small Business Association Web site at www.sba.gov/starting

CLIA

CLIA Regulations: www.hcfa.gov/medicaid/clia/cliahome.htm
CLIA categories: ftp.cdc.gov/pub/laboratory_info/clia

CODING

CPT codebook: www.ama-assn.org
ICD codebook: www.ama-assn.org or www.cdc.gov/nchs/icd9.htm
Guidelines for E/M Coding: www.hcfa.gov/audience/planprov.htm

EDUCATION OF STAFF

Correspondence courses in medical office management, functions: www.baker.edu/catalog/new/med.html

FAIR LABOR STANDARDS AND EQUAL EMPLOYMENT OPPORTUNITY

Fair Labor Standards Act: (Department of Labor Web site): www.dol.gov
Equal Employment Opportunity Laws: www.eeoc.gov/laws.html
U.S. Equal Employment Opportunity Commission (EEOC): www.eeoc.gov

FEDERAL TRADE COMMISSION

Truth in advertising, restraint of trade: www.ftc.gov

FRAUD AND ABUSE

Fraud and Abuse: www.hcfa.gov, www.hcfa.gov/medicare/fraud, www.ama-assn.org, www.hcfa.gov/audience/planprov.htm
Fraud and Abuse, penalties: www.ama-assn.org/physlegl/legal/doc1d.htm, anti-kickback: www.dhhs.gov/progorg/oig/ak/safenr.htm
Compliance: (HHS Web site): www.hhs.gov; other compliance Web sites: Corporate Compliance Home Page at www.corporatecompliance.com, Compliance Programs and the Corporate Sentencing Guidelines at www.carswell.com/records/CPG.html, Office of Inspector General at www.sbanonline.sba.gov/ignet/internal/hhs/hhs.html, Health Care Financing Administration at www.hcfa.gov, qui tam case information by Taxpayers Against

Fraud at www.taf.org, Federal Register's Web site at www.access.gpo.gov/su_docs/aces/aces140.html, Florida Medicare Web site at www.floridamedicare.com

HEALTH CARE FINANCING ADMINISTRATION

(HCFA): www.hcfa.gov

INFECTION CONTROL

Universal Precautions, recommendations for prevention of HIV in health care settings: CDC Web site at www.phppo.cdc.gov

INSURANCE

Insurance, Liability: Evaluating a liability insurance policy: www.ama-assn.org/physlegl/legal/profins.htm

LEGAL AND ETHICAL ISSUES

Legal Issues and AMA Policies on Ethics: www.ama-assn.org
AMA Current Opinions on Medical and Legal Issues: www.ama-assn.org/physlegl/legal/patphys.htm
AMA Code of Medical Ethics: www.ama-assn.org/physlegl/legal/patphys.htm

LICENSES, DEA

DEA License; Prescribing Controlled Substances; Controlled Substances Schedule: www.deadiversion.usdoj.gov/drugreg/process.htm
DEA Homepage: www.usdoj.gov/dea
DEA Schedules I-V: www.usdoj.gov/dea/directory.htm

LICENSES, STATE MEDICAL

State medical licensing boards or boards of medical examiners: www.mednets.com/usmedlicensing.htm

AMA Web site for basics on getting a license and for links to state medical boards: www.amaassn.org/ama/pub/category/2644.html
National Board of Medical Examiners (NBME): www.nbme.org
Federation Licensing Examination (FLEX): www.fsmb.org
Educational Commission for Foreign Medical Graduates (ECFMG): www.ecfmg.org

LOCATING AN OFFICE

Chambers of Commerce: www.uschamber.com

MEDICARE AND MEDICAID

HCFA Medicare, Medicaid Web site: www.hcfa.gov/medicare/medicare.htm
Medicare: Medigap, Medicare+Choice: www.medicare.gov/Choices/Overview.asp
Medicaid: www.hcfa.gov/medicaid/medicaid.htm for information about Medicaid.
Medicaid: state Medicaid directors and addresses: medicaid.aphsa.org/members.htm
Blue Cross/Blue Shield: www.bluecares.com
EIN number, tax information for small businesses: www.irs.gov

PRINTED INFORMATION

Printed information on health issues, NIH, medical issues, OSHA: Government Printing Office at www.access.gpo.gov

SETTING UP PRACTICE

AMA Young Physicians Publications List (AMA-YPS): www.ama-assn.org. Information on board certification, preparation of a curriculum vitae, job search tips, what you need to know about contracts, resources for entering practice, and managed care.

About the Author

Rebecca B. Campen obtained an M.D. at the Medical College of Georgia in 1987, a J.D. at the University of Georgia School of Law in 1983, and completed a residency in dermatology at the Medical College of Georgia in 1991. She is a Fellow of the American Academy of Dermatology, has served as a member of the Regulatory Committee of the American Academy of Dermatology and as Liaison to the Federal Trade Commission. She has participated in forums at her specialty conferences on subjects including protection against malpractice and compliance with federal regulations. During her career as a dermatologist, Dr. Campen has practiced in many different offices in many different practice arrangements. She set up and established her own private dermatology office in Grosse Pointe, Michigan and was affiliated with Harness, Dickey, and Pierce, a patent and trademark law firm in Bloomfield Hills, Michigan. She was a member of the clinical faculty of Louisiana State University Medical School, where she served as Director of Compliance of the Louisiana State University HealthCare Network. She is currently a member of the faculty of the Department of Dermatology, Harvard Medical School, where she has served as Chief of Staff of the Department of Dermatology. At present, she is a practicing member of Dermatology Associates at Massachusetts General Hospital, a member of the Executive Committee of the Department of Dermatology at Harvard Medical School, and the Deputy Director of the Massachusetts General Hospital/Harvard Cutaneous Biology Research Center. She serves as chairman of the Quality Assurance Committee of the Massachusetts General Hospital Department of Dermatology. She is a member of the Massachusetts General Hospital Trustees Compliance Committee and the Massachusetts General Hospital Patient Care Assessment Committee.

Index

Academic medicine, 105–106
Accounting, 16–17, 36. *See also* Billing.
   financial reports for, 72
   insurance and, 102–103
   officer manager and, 29
   payroll, 26–27, 31–32, 36
   petty cash, 71–72
   safeguards for, 48
   sole proprietorships and, 31–32
Accreditation, 91
Advanced cardiac life support (ACLS), 46
Advertising
   employment, 31, 45
   phone book, 25–26
   of practice, 32
   truth in, 93
Age discrimination, 49, 87
AIDS, 92–93
Allergies, 64
American Medical Association (AMA), 73
   legal advice and, 98
   liability insurance and, 103
   OSHA regulations and, 92–93
   Young Physicians Publications of, 37
Americans with Disabilities Act (ADA), 77
Answering service, 26, 43
Anti-kickback regulations, 88
Anti-reassignment regulations, 87–88
Assignment of benefits, 64, 70
Attorney
   for equipment leases, 42
   for job contract, 10–12
   for malpractice suits, 99–100
   for managed care contracts, 53
   for mergers, 93–94
Autoclaves, 42–43, 46

Basic life support (BLS), 46
Benefits
   academic medicine, 105–106
   assignment of, 64, 70
   employment, 7, 9, 10
   determination of, 45–46
Billing, 16, 32. *See also* Accounting; Collections.
   coding for, 57–60, 66, 87
   co-payments and, 67, 86, 88
   officer manager and, 29
   procedures for, 68–70, 86–87
   software for, 40–41
   unbundling for, 86
Blue Cross, 24–25, 53–54
   fees for, 30
Brochures, patient, 22–23, 64
Business plan, 13, 27

Cancellations, appointment, 47
Cash flow, 16, 27–28
   insurance for, 102
Certificates of proficiency, 24
Certification of necessity, 23
Chaperones, 67–68
Charting, 29, 41, 64–67. *See also* Medical records.
   audits of, 57, 85, 98
   dictating and, 22, 66
   difficult patients and, 82
Civil Rights Act, 49
Claims made insurance, 9, 101
Clinical Laboratory Improvement Amendments (CLIA), 15, 23, 35
   licensing by, 42, 90–91
   staff training and, 46
Coding, 57–60, 66, 87
   books for, 27, 30, 33–34
Collections, 69–70. *See also* Billing.
   agency for, 29–30, 33, 69

117

Competition, 14. *See also* Non-compete clause.
Compliance, 85–94
 certificate of, 91
 plan for, 89
Computer systems, 17, 23, 40–41, 68–69
 leasing of, 42
Consent
 informed, 22, 29, 34, 97–98
 to transfer records, 97
Consolidated Omnibus Budget Reconciliation Act (COBRA), 88
Consultations, 58–59, 71
Continuing Medical Education (CME), 77, 88
Contracts
 employment, 8–12
 managed care, 51–56
Controlled substances, 19, 52, 75–76, 88
Co-payments, 67, 86
 waiving of, 88
Cosmetic procedures, 86, 93
CPT codebook, 27, 30, 33–34, 59

DEA (Drug Enforcement Administration) license, 19, 52, 75–76, 88
Deductibles, Medicare, 70, 86, 88
Department of Health and Human Services (DHHS), 55, 90
Department of Labor, 48
Diagnosis codes, 27, 30, 33–34. *See also* Coding.
Diagnosis-related group (DRG), 54–55
Dictating, 22, 66
Difficult patients, 81–84, 100, 107–108
Disability insurance, 102
Disabled patients, 49, 77
Discrimination, 49, 87
Doctor-patient relationship, 97–99
Drug Enforcement Administration (DEA) license, 19, 52, 75–76, 88
Drugs. *See also* Pharmaceutical representatives.
 abuse of, 76
 patients seeking, 81–82
 side effects of, 82

Educational Commission for Foreign Medical Graduates Exam (ECFMG), 19
Embezzlement, 47–48, 101
Emergencies, 46, 75
Employee identification number (EIN), 25
Employees, 45–49. *See also* Jobs.
 advertising for, 31, 45
 hiring of, 29, 31
 incentive pay for, 47
 independent contractors vs., 10
 payroll for, 26–27, 31–32, 36
 physicians as, 7–12
  advantages of, 3–5
  rotation of, 46
  temporary, 33
  training of, 46–47, 72, 75, 83, 87
  trial period for, 35
Encounter form, 29, 30, 34
Equal employment opportunity laws, 48–49
Equipment, 16, 21–22, 39–44
 dictating, 22
 emergency, 46, 75
 for exam rooms, 41–42
 leasing of, 42
 maintenance of, 42
 ordering of, 30
Equity, in practice, 9
Ethical issues, 73, 89
 liability and, 97–100
Evaluation and management (E/M) codes, 57–60
Evaluations, patient, 47
Exam rooms, 65–66
 equipment for, 41–42

Fair Labor Standards Act, 48
Federal Licensing Exam (FLEX), 19
Federal Trade Commission (FTC), 93–94
Feedback, patient, 34, 47–48, 73
Fee schedule, 30, 52
Filing system, 29, 40

118 GOING INTO MEDICAL PRACTICE

Financial reports, 72. See also
    Accounting.
Fire safety, 43–44
FLEX (Federal Licensing Exam), 19
Forms, 22, 29, 52–53
    patient, 64
Fraud, 85–88
FTC (Federal Trade Commission),
    93–94
Furniture, 16, 21, 39–40. See also
    Equipment.

Gag rules, 53
Gatekeepers, 51–52

Hazardous waste disposal, 29
Health Care Financing Administration
    (HCFA), 55. See also
    Medicare.
    audits by, 57, 85, 98
    coding for, 57–60, 66, 87
    forms of, 23, 68
    fraud and, 85–88
Health Insurance Claim Form, 23
Health maintenance organizations
    (HMOs), 25, 51
Hepatitis vaccination, 46, 92
HIV disease, 92–93
Hospital
    privileges at, 23–24
    rounds at, 74, 78

ICD codebook, 27, 30, 33–34, 59
Incentive pay, 8–9, 47
Incorporation, 31
Independent contractors, 10
Informed consent, 34, 97–98
    forms for, 22, 29
Insurance, 13, 31, 64, 101–103
    malpractice, 9–10, 16, 27, 101
Medigap, 54
    rejected claims and, 69–70
    types of, 101–103
Internal Revenue Service (IRS), 25
International Classification of Disease
    (ICD) codebook, 27, 30,
    33–34, 59
Interviews, 8

Jobs. See also Employees.
    advertising for, 31, 45
    contract for, 8–12
    descriptions of, 31, 41
    discrimination and, 49, 87
    interview for, 8
    search for, 3–5

Kickbacks, 88

Laboratory tests, 42–43
    CLIA license for, 42, 90–91
    specimen submission forms for,
    23, 29
Lawyer. See Attorney.
Leases
    equipment, 42
    office, 28–29
Legal issues, 97–100. See also
    Attorney.
Liability, 97–100
    insurance for, 101–103
License
    CLIA, 42, 90–91
    medical, 14–15, 19–20
Loan applications, 13, 27–28
Location, of practice, 3, 14, 20–21

Maintenance agreements, 42
Malpractice, 99–100. See also
    Negligence.
    insurance for, 9–10, 16, 27, 101
Managed care, 7, 107
    contracts for, 51–56
    forms for, 52–53
Medicaid, 55–56
    fees for, 30
    provider for, 25
    regulations with, 85–89
Medical assistant, duties of, 41,
    66–67
Medical license, 14–15, 19–20
Medical records, 40. See also Charting.
    alterations to, 99
    coding for, 57–60, 66, 87
    insurance for, 101–102
    after office closure, 98
    transfers of, 97

Medicare, 54–55
  deductibles for, 70, 86, 88
  fees for, 30
  provider for, 23–24
  regulations with, 85–89
Medicare+Choice, 54
Medicine, academic, 105–106
Medigap insurance, 54
Medisoft Web site, 40
Mental problems of patients, 34–35, 82–83
Mission statement, 89
Moving expenses, 9
Music system, 44

National Board of Medical Examiners Exam (NBME), 19
Negligence, 82, 99. See also Malpractice.
Negotiations, 12. See also Contracts.
Non-compete clause, 11–12, 14
No-shows, 47

Occupational Safety and Health Administration. See OSHA regulations.
Occurrence-based insurance, 9, 101
Office manager, 45
  duties of, 29–30
  safeguards with, 47–48, 75
Office of Inspector General (OIG), 89
Office procedures, 63–78
  policy manual for, 72–73, 83, 89
On-call duties, 11, 74
OSHA regulations, 15, 35, 42–43, 67
  AMA training kit for, 92–93
  compliance with, 91–93
  staff training and, 46
Overhead insurance, 102

Pagers, 23, 33
Partnerships, 31
Patients
  angry, 83–84
  chaperones for, 67–68
  difficult, 81–84, 100, 107–108
  disabled, 49, 77
  drug-seeking, 81–82
  education of, 76
  encounter form for, 29, 30, 34
  evaluation by, 47
  feedback from, 34, 47–48, 73
  information sheet for, 22–23, 30–31, 64
  interactions with, 33–34
  office procedures for, 63–78
  physician's relationship with, 97–99
  psychological problems of, 34–35, 82–83
  referral of, 53, 58–59, 71, 88
  terminating care of, 97–98
Payroll, 26–27, 31–32, 36. See also Salaries.
Peer review organizations (PROs), 55
Petty cash, 71–72. See also Accounting.
Pharmaceutical representatives, 43, 74. See also Drugs.
Phone systems, 25–26, 42, 43
Physical disabilities, 49, 77
Physician (s)
  calls from, 71, 75
  as employees, 7–12
  advantages of, 3–5
  fraud by, 85–88
  on-call, 11, 74
  patient relationship with, 97–99
  personal, 34–35
  primary care, 51
Physician hospital organizations (PHO), 51
Point of service organizations, 51
Policy manual, 72–73, 83, 89
Potassium hydroxide preparations, 90
PPM (provider-performed microscopy), 90–91
PPOs (preferred provider organizations), 25, 51
PPS (prospective payment system), 54–55
Practice
  academic vs. private, 105–106
  closing of, 98
  equity in, 0

120 GOING INTO MEDICAL PRACTICE

insurance for, 101–103
location of, 3, 14, 20–21
plans, 19–37
purchase of, 5
rent by, 10–11
rent for, 20–21, 28–29
safeguards for, 47–48, 75
set-up costs for, 13–17
types of, 7
Preferred provider organizations (PPOs), 25, 51
Prescriptions, 81–82
Procedures
  codes for, 59–60
  policy manual for, 72–73, 83, 89
  room for, 42
Productivity measures, 11
Professional courtesy, 88
Proficiency attestations, 24
Progress notes, 22, 65. See also Medical records.
PROs (peer review organizations), 55
Prospective payment system (PPS), 54–55
Provider-performed microscopy (PPM), 90–91
Psychological problems of patients, 34–35, 82–83
Public relations, 24, 35
Public service opportunities, 15, 24, 35, 78

Quality assurance (QA), 35, 77
Questionnaires, 22

Rage, patient, 83–84
Reassignment regulations, 87–88
Reception area, 39–40, 64
Records. See Medical records.
Recruiters, 7
Referrals, patient, 53, 58–59, 71, 88
Relative value scale (RVS), 55
Rent
  by practice, 10–11
  for practice, 20–21, 28–29
Retirement plans, 9, 105
Rounds, hospital, 74, 78

Safety, 43–44. See also OSHA regulations.
Salaries, 8–9, 13. See also Payroll.
  determination of, 45–46
  gender-disparate, 49
Scheduling, 26, 32, 63
  cancellations and, 47
  problems with, 47, 82–83
  wave, 70–71
Self-employment, 3–5
  steps toward, 19–37
Set-up costs, 13–17
Sick time, 9
Small Business Association, 25
Software. See Computer systems.
Sole proprietorship, 31
Sound system, 44
Speaking engagements, 15, 24, 35, 78
Specimen submission forms, 23, 29
Staff. See Employees.
Stress, 34–35
Substance abuse, 76
Supplies. See Equipment.
Support staff, 9

Tail coverage, 9–10, 101
Telephones. See Phone systems.
Temporary help, 33
Time management, 83
Trade, restraint of, 93–94
Training, staff, 46–47, 72, 75, 83, 87

Unbundling, 86
Unemployment compensation, 48
Unique Physician Identification Number (UPIN), 59
Universal precautions, 42, 43, 46, 92–93

Vaccinations, hepatitis, 46, 92
Volunteer opportunities, 35

Waiting room, 39, 63–64
Wave scheduling, 70–71
Workers compensation, 101

Young Physicians Publications, 37